MW00527694

Paradoxes of Time

in

Saint Augustine

The Aquinas Lecture, 1996

Paradoxes of Time
in
Saint Augustine

Under the auspices of the
Wisconsin-Alpha Chapter of Phi Sigma Tau

by

Roland J. Teske, S.J.

MARQUETTE
UNIVERSITY

PRESS

Library of Congress Cataloging-in-Publication Data

Teske, Roland J., 1934-
    Paradoxes of time in Saint Augustine / by Roland J. Teske.
      p. cm. — (The Aquinas lecture ; 1996)
    Includes bibliographical references.
    ISBN 0-87462-163-1 (pbk.)
    1. Time—History. 2. Augustine, Saint, Bishop of Hippo—
    Contributions in doctrine of time. I. Title. II. Series.
B655.Z7T47 1996
115'.092—dc20   95-50197

© 1996 Marquette University Press

Printed in the United States of America

MARQUETTE UNIVERSITY PRESS
MILWAUKEE

The Association of Jesuit University Presses

Prefatory

The Wisconsin-Alpha Chapter of Phi Sigma Tau, the International Honor Society for Philosophy at Marquette University, each year invites a scholar to deliver a lecture in honor of St. Thomas Aquinas.

The 1996 Aquinas Lecture, *Paradoxes of Time in St. Augustine*, was delivered in the Tony and Lucille Weasler Auditorium on Sunday, February 25, 1996, by the Reverend Roland J. Teske, S.J., Professor of Philosophy at Marquette University.

Fr. Teske was born in Milwaukee and upon graduation from Marquette University High School entered the Society of Jesus in 1952. After completing his undergraduate work at Saint Louis University, he also earned an M.A. in classics at Saint Louis University and a licentiate degree in sacred theology at St. Mary's College, St. Marys, Kansas. He pursued doctoral studies in philosophy at the University of Toronto, which awarded him the Ph.D. in 1973. Since 1970 he has taught mainly at Marquette University, where he became full professor in 1990. He has also served as acting dean of the College of Philosophy and Letters at Saint Louis University and as visiting professor at Santa Clara University, and he has held the Edmund Miller, S.J. Chair in Classics at John Carroll University.

Under a grant from the National Endowment for the Humanities, Fr. Teske has translated two volumes of Augustine: *St. Augustine: On Genesis. Two Books on Genesis Against the Manichees and On the Literal Interpretation of Genesis: An Unfinished Book* (1991); and *St. Augustine: Arianism and Other Heresies* (1995). He is currently translating Augustine's anti-Pelagian writings under a grant from the Augustinian Heritage Institute. He has also co-edited *Augustine: Presbyter Factus Sum* (1993); has translated *William of Auvergne: The Immortality of the Soul* (1991), and *Henry of Ghent: Disputed Questions on Free Will* (1993); and has co-translated *The Trinity* by William of Auvergne (1989), and *The Spiritual Writings of Robert Bellarmine* (1989).

Fr. Teske is also the author of nearly fifty studies in the history of philosophy, including over thirty on Augustine. Among these are: "Ultimate Reality according to Augustine of Hippo," "Augustine, Maximinus, and Imagination," "Saint Augustine as Philosopher: The Birth of Christian Metaphysics," "The *De Libero Arbitrio* Proof for the Existence of God," "Divine Immutability in St. Augustine," "Saint Augustine on the Incorporeality of the Soul in Letter 166," and "Augustine, Flew and the Free Will Defense."

To Fr. Teske's distinguished list of publications, Phi Sigma Tau is pleased to add: *Paradoxes of Time in Saint Augustine*.

PARADOXES OF TIME
IN
SAINT AUGUSTINE

by

ROLAND J. TESKE, S.J.

For the many who have taught me,
but especially in memory of
George P. Klubertanz, S.J.,
Gerald Van Ackeren, S.J., and
Francis C. Wade, S.J.

Paradoxes of Time

in

Saint Augustine

Augustine's quip in Book Eleven of the *Confessions* that, if no one asks him, he knows what time is, but if he wants to explain it to someone who asks him, he does not know, is perhaps the least paradoxical of the many paradoxical things that Augustine does say on the subject of time.[1] Book Eleven of the *Confessions* brims with paradoxes and problems, some of which Augustine resolved or at least believed that he had resolved, while others are left unresolved — or their resolution is at least not apparent. In this lecture I want to examine three paradoxes or puzzles in Book Eleven of the *Confessions*. Each of these paradoxes concerns time, and the resolution of each of them, I shall argue, is tied to what Augustine learned from the great Neoplatonist philosopher, Plotinus.

The first paradox arises from the skeptical question about what God was doing before he made heaven and earth. Augustine's answer could hardly be more paradoxical; he said that there was no time when God did nothing, since there was no time before God created heaven and earth. The second paradox arises from his attempt to discover what time is. Since the past is no longer and the future is not yet, there is only present time. But the present has no extent, because the part of the present day, hour, or minute that is past is no more and the part that is future is not yet. On the other hand, though neither the past nor the future are and the present passes in an instant, Augustine claims that we do measure time and that measuring time presupposes that time has some extent. Indeed, he eventually comes to a definition of time as a distention of the mind or soul, a definition which is itself a puzzle and even more of a puzzle in view of his claims that only the present exists and that it has no extent. The third paradox arises from the fact that Augustine both defines time as a distention of the mind — so that it would seem that time could not exist before there were human minds — and, nonetheless, explicitly claims that there was time before human beings existed. That is, he seems to hold that time is both something subjective and private to each individual human being and something objective and public for all human beings. Though at times he seems to give two quite different accounts of what time is, in Book Eleven he speaks as though he were seeking "the power and nature of time,"[2] that is, a definition of time without qualification rather than a definition of a particular sort of time.

Before turning to these three paradoxes or puzzles about time, I would like to begin with several prenotes. First of all, Augustine's discussion of time occurs within the context of the whole of the *Confessions*. To isolate the paradoxes about time from the rest of this great work of art runs the risk of distorting what Augustine had in mind in the work as a whole. On the other hand, if one can get clear about what is going on in Book Eleven, it is possible that one may also become clearer about the whole work. While almost everyone acknowledges that the *Confessions* is a classic and an artistic masterpiece, there is little agreement about how its thirteen books form a unified whole.[3] The first nine books seem somewhat autobiographical, while Book Ten focuses upon Augustine's state of soul at the time of its composition, and then the remaining three books form a commentary on the first chapter of the Book of Genesis, a commentary which by Book Thirteen becomes wildly allegorical, beyond almost anything else in Augustine's works.[4] A careful examination of the paradoxes of time will, I hope, provide some insight into how the thirteen books of the *Confessions* constitute a unified work of art.

Second, in Book Eleven Augustine is commenting on scripture, specifically on the hexaemeron, the six days of creation in Genesis 1. Though an exercise in biblical exegesis hardly seems to be a task for a philosopher or for a lecture in philosophy, what Augustine does in this book is, I contend, quite philosophical. First of all, it owes, as I hope to convince you, very much to the great Neoplatonist philosopher, Plotinus, whose *Enneads* Augustine read in the months before his baptism in the church of Milan at the Easter vigil on April 24, 387.[5] In this respect Book Eleven is perhaps the most philosophical book of the whole of the *Confessions.* Secondly, Augustine does not use scripture merely as a source of "proof-texts," but rather as point of departure in the quest for understanding.[6] John Rist compares Augustine's use of scripture to the contemporary philosopher's use of premises or models generated by thought-experiments. He argues, "To attempt to make sense of Augustine's thought without taking such theological models at least as seriously as one takes a modern philosopher's models is to emasculate the thought itself, and to deprive Augustine of his philosophical integrity."[7] Hence, the emphasis in Book Eleven rests upon coming to an understanding of such biblical premises or models — an understanding that, I shall argue, owes at least as much to Plotinus as it does to the scriptures.

Third, the *Confessions* is a work of piety and perhaps even of mysticism, but it was certainly not Augustine's idea — nor, I would add, is it a sound idea — that piety should preclude the role of the intellect. A highly regarded German theologian has claimed, "The *Confessions* are prayer, a conversation in chorus of the community that joins in prayer; the person whom they move to join in prayer has understood what is essential in them."[8] But to make participation in prayer — without any qualification — the essence of the *Confessions* overlooks the fact that, when Augustine prays in the *Confessions*, he most often prays for understanding.[9] He was well aware that one could be a good Christian while remaining at the level of simple faith, at the level of the "little ones" in the Church who had to be fed on milk, but he certainly did not think that one ought to remain a little one in the faith through all of one's life.[10] Later Consentius, a budding theologian who wrote to Augustine, asking for help in understanding the Trinity, found him too philosophical. He admonished Augustine that "one ought to derive the truth from faith rather than reason" and argued that "if the faith of the Church were grasped by the method of argument rather than by the piety of belief, no one but philosophers and rhetoricians would attain beatitude."[11] In replying to the young man, Augustine admonished him in turn, "Have a great love for understanding."[12] In his *Retractationes*, moreover, Augustine describes the effect his *Confessions* had on him both when he wrote it and when he reread it — the same effect that he hoped it would have on his readers, namely, that it would arouse both the intellect and the affections toward God.[13] I hope to convince you, as I am convinced, that Augustine's discussion of the paradoxes of time was directed toward serious intellectual problems and their resolution rather than toward merely bringing one to enter into prayer.[14]

A final prenote — Augustine employs not merely paradox, but prayer as a means of speculative en-

quiry. The opening paragraphs of the *Confessions*,
for example, present the readers with the paradox
of divine omnipresence in the form of a prayer. Augustine tries to get his readers intellectually involved
through the use of a technique referred to as
exercitatio animi — an exercise for the mind — so
that they are brought to grasp the non-bodily presence of God who is whole everywhere, that is, to
grasp that God is everywhere and that all of God is
wherever he is. He does this by getting us to puzzle
over how we can invite God into our hearts, since,
if he were not already there, we would not even be.[15]
Though prayer is hardly a form of philosophical dis-
course much in vogue today, Augustine found a pre-
cedent for such prayer in Plotinus who said, "Let us
speak of [the One] in this way, first invoking God
himself, not in spoken words, but stretching our-
selves out with our soul into prayer to him, able in
this way to pray alone to him alone."[16] Peter Brown
goes so far as to claim that in late antiquity "prayer
…was a recognized vehicle for speculative enquiry."[17]
It was, however, more often used as a preliminary
move to lift the mind to God. But prayers, Brown
admits, "had never been used, as Augustine would
use them throughout the *Confessions* to strike up a
lively conversation with Him." He cites Dodds' fa-
mous line: "Plotinus never gossiped with the One
as Augustine gossips in the *Confessions*."[18] Yet, if Augustine was engaged in gossiping with his God, it
was, I contend, a very intelligent sort of gossip meant

for our intellectual and spiritual exercise far more than what the term "gossip" would normally convey.

The bibliography on Augustine's account of time grows at a startling pace, and the divergent interpretations of what Augustine understood by time indicates that on many points there is no unanimity present in Augustinian scholarship.[19] By this lecture I shall certainly add to the bibliography; I shall also, I hope, point out some of the paradoxes and puzzles in what Augustine says about time. Whether I bring any clarity to the subject or resolve any of the problems must remain as yet an open question.

I. The First Paradox

In 427 or 428, when Augustine was over seventy years old and had been bishop of Hippo Regius for over thirty years, he wrote one of the most unusual works in the history of philosophy or theology, his *Retractationes*. In that work he reviewed all of his books — to his surprise he found two hundred and thirty-two of them.[20] The Latin title *Retractationes* can be misleading, since he certainly did not — at least primarily — *retract* what he had written; rather, he explained, defended, and warned against misinterpreting what he had said; only rarely did he admit that he has been rash or mistaken.[21] In commenting on the thirteen books of his *Confessions* he said, "The first to the tenth books were written about me; the remaining three are about the holy scriptures from the words, 'In the beginning God made heaven and earth' up to the rest on the Sabbath."[22] Hence, in Augustine's own mind, Book Eleven of the *Confessions* marked a turning point in the whole work. At the beginning of the book, he prays in words that have misled some to suppose that he was about to comment on the whole of the Bible:[23] "Let me confess to you whatever I shall find in your books … and consider the marvels of your law, from the very beginning in which you made heaven and earth, even to the everlasting reign of your holy city with you."[24] Books Eleven through Thirteen contain Augustine's third commentary on the beginning of Genesis in which, especially in the final book, he interprets the six days of creation as prophetic of the whole history of salvation.[25]

Book Eleven of the *Confessions*, then, begins an examination of the Genesis account of the six days of creation, and in the whole six thousand plus words of the book Augustine never gets beyond verse one: "In the beginning God made heaven and earth." In fact, he does not finish his exegesis of this verse in Book Eleven, for he spends most of Book Twelve on the meaning of the heaven mentioned in that verse.[26] He begins Book Eleven, puzzling over whether God to whom he is speaking comes to learn in time what he says to God in time and over why Augustine speaks to him in time, if God already knows what Augustine is going to say. In commenting on Genesis 1:1, he first guides his readers to some understanding, largely by way of negation, of how God created the heaven and the earth. God did not make heaven and earth out of some already existing stuff, but out of nothing; he did not make heaven and earth in some place or at some time, because before he made heaven and earth, there was no place where he might make them and no time at which he might make them. He did not, moveover, make heaven and earth by speaking some words whose syllables sound one after the other, for words that sound in time presuppose the existence of creatures; rather, he made heaven and earth by his eternal Word.[27]

1. The Skeptical Question

In chapter ten Augustine turns to an objection raised against the Genesis account of creation. The objection asks, "What was God doing before he made heaven and earth?"[28] The question is repeated both when Augustine tells his reader the answer he is not going to give to that question and at the end of the book where he adds the further question: "Why did it enter [God's] mind to make something when he previously never made anything?"[29] The fact that the question brackets the whole discussion of time indicates the importance of the question, which does pose serious intellectual problems. It not only presents one with the very anthropomorphic picture of a God who had spent ages upon ages doing nothing, then went into a feverish pitch of work for six days, and finally returned to his rest on the seventh. The question also presupposes that God himself changed, first not willing to create and then suddenly willing to do so. The question's presupposition runs counter one of Augustine's most basic convictions: the absolute immutability of God.

In what I like to call the prime analogate of divine illumination, Augustine came to see that God is utterly immutable. At the beginning of Book Seven of the *Confessions*, he says to God,

> I believed with the very marrow of my bones that you are incorruptible and inviolable and immutable. Though I did not know whence or how, I clearly saw and was certain that what can be corrupted is inferior to what cannot be corrupted, and I unhesitatingly placed what cannot be violated above what is violable, and I saw that what suffers no change is better than what can be changed.[30]

In *Letter* 18, which he wrote in 390 to his friend, Celestine, Augustine describes in a nutshell his three-tiered view of reality. At the lowest level there is "a nature that can change in both place and time, such as a body." Next comes "a nature that can in no sense change in place, but can change in time, such as the soul." Finally, at the top of the hierarchy there is "a nature that cannot change in either place or in time, and that is God."[31] Hence, whatever is in any way subject to change is a creature, while the creator is utterly immutable.[32]

The answer to the skeptical question that Augustine says he will not give is better known than the

answer he does give. He says that he will not give
the answer someone reportedly gave, avoiding the
objection by pouring ridicule on the one who asked
it, namely, "He was preparing hell for people who
pry into such deep matters."[33] That answer which
he does not give strikes us as a joke, but Augustine
is quite serious, I believe. For that answer was most
likely a sample of the sort of response that he himself had received when, as a young man with intellectual problems, he brought his own questions to
the African clergy. These men, it seems, were themselves not well educated.[34] It seems, moreover, that
they silenced those with intellectual problems by de-
manding blind faith — even when the object to be
believed seemed clearly impossible.[35] In an early
work Augustine reminds Honoratus, a friend whom
he had led into Manichaeism, that they had fallen
in with those people only because the Manichees
"claimed that, having set aside the terror of authority, they would by pure and simple reason lead to
God those willing to listen to them and that they
would set them free from all error."[36] He recalls how
for nine years he spurned the religion of his mother
"as old wives' tales" and followed those men because
they claimed that "we were terrified by superstition
and had faith imposed upon us before reason."[37] He
reminds Honoratus of how the Manichees "blame
the Catholic Church especially because she com-
mands those who come to her to believe, whereas
they boast that they do not impose the yoke of belief, but open the fountain of doctrine."[38] The anti-

intellectualism of the African church drove the young
Augustine from the faith, and its effect upon Augustine still stands as a clear warning for the Church of
today that the minds of some of the most intelligent
young women and men can easily be driven from the
Church by a similar anti-intellectualism.[39]

Who are the people who posed this objection? The
proximate source is surely the Manichees, those cu-
rious folk who spread the dualistic gnostic religion
of Mani from its native Persia throughout the Medi-
terranean basin and as far east as China. They accounted
for the evil in this present age of the world in terms of
a conflict in the beginning times between the two first
principles, Good and Evil, or the Kingdoms of Light
and of Darkness. As a result of that conflict the present
world, including each of us, is a mixture of good and
evil, of light and darkness, so that each of us is a battle-
field and our present life is a struggle to set free our
good or divine self from our evil self.[40]

The story of Augustine's nine years as a Hearer, or
layman, in the Manichaean sect is well known.[41] The
Confessions recounts his escape from their clutches,
largely through the discovery of Christian Neoplatonism in the church of Milan, where he found that
not all members of the Catholic Church thought of
God in crudely anthropomorphic terms and where
he learned to think of God and the soul as non-
bodily realities. What all too often is forgotten is
that Augustine was the first thinker in the Western
Church clearly to formulate the concepts of God
and of the soul as non-bodily beings.[42] In fact, he so

successfully taught the West to think of God as non-bodily that many presuppose that the doctrine is to be found even in the biblical revelation.[43] Once he had come under the influence of the Neoplatonists and had learned to conceive of God as non-bodily, Augustine was able to answer the question with which the Manichees loved to torment the Catholics, "Where does evil come from?" From Plotinus he learned that he had first to answer the question, "What is evil?" before attempting to answer the question about the source of evil.[44] Augustine admitted in the *Confessions* that his inability to conceive of a non-bodily substance was the source of almost all of his intellectual difficulties and was the reason for his belief that evil was a bodily substance.[45] And it is easy to see that, if whatever is real is a body, then God is a body, and if evil is real, it too is a body. But then either evil exists in God, or God is limited by evil, if evil exists outside of God. That is, if one thinks of God as a bodily being and if there is evil, which must also be a body, one has to admit either that there is evil in God or that God is not infinite.[46]

That Augustine was able to resolve the problem of evil posed by the Manichees, at least to his own satisfaction and to that of many in the Christian tradition, in terms of a privation of positive reality is well known. But what is not as well known is that the other Manichaean question, "What was God doing before he made heaven and earth?" required a correlative Neoplatonic insight into God's existence as eternal — eternal not merely in the sense of having neither beginning nor end, but also in the sense of having no succession of either past or future so that there is only the abiding present. A verbal solution to the question is easy, but to grasp the idea of the all-at-onceness of divine eternity is no mean intellectual task. As to conceive of God and the soul as non-bodily realities involved transcending what can be imagined or pictured in the mind, so to conceive of God as always present and whole all at once demands a transcendence of anything one can mentally picture.

Augustine had faced the Manichaean objection about what God was doing before he made heaven and earth in his first commentary on Genesis, *De Genesi contra Manichaeos.* The Manichees had posed the question in two forms. The first form of the question asked, "If God made heaven and earth in some beginning in time, what was he doing before he made heaven and earth?"[47] The second form of the question asked, "And why did he suddenly decide to do what he had never before done for eternal times?[48] Edward Peters has labeled the two forms of the question respectively as the *quid antequam* form and the *cur non antea* form.[49] He has traced the latter form to the Epicureans and the former to the Gnostics and has suggested that it was some Gnostic who

> found by turning the *cur non antea* Epicurean question into a *quid antequam* form he could indict the Old Testament creation story and the Christian doctrine of Christ as Logos and at the

same time imply a secret knowledge of exactly what that "God" was doing before he created the heavens and the earth.[50]

In the *Confessions* the objectors spell out the basis of their objection. If God had been taking his ease and had not made anything, why did he not continue to take his ease thereafter, just as he had previously abstained from any work. After all, if there came about in him a new decision to create that had not been there before, he would have changed and would not be truly eternal. On the other hand, if God always willed that creatures exist, why did creatures not always exist?[51]

Augustine's answer to the question in the *Confessions* is quite in accord with his early answer in *De Genesi contra Manichaeos.* He insists that time is a creature of God and that before God created anything there was no time. Hence, there was no time when God made nothing. "You made time itself, and times could not pass before you made times. But if there was no time before heaven and earth, why do they ask what you did then? There was no 'then' when there was no time."[52] In order for Augustine to be able to give the answer that he gave, he had to have a concept of God's being as timeless. Otherwise, he could not say that there was no time when God did not create anything.[53] That is, just as he was unable to answer the Manichaean question, "Where does evil come from?" without the concept of God as a non-bodily substance that is whole everywhere (*totus ubique*), so he could not solve the other Manichaean question, "What was God doing before he made heaven and earth?" without the concept of God as a non-temporal being or as whole all at once (*totus simul*).

2. The Concept of Divine Eternity and its Source

Key to Augustine's being able to answer the Manichaean objection is his concept of divine eternity as timeless. That Augustine did come to a concept of divine eternity as timelessness is beyond dispute. A few texts, mainly from the *Confessions*, illustrate how he formulated that difficult concept. In speaking of God's Word by which God created heaven and earth, he says that

> it is spoken everlastingly and all things are everlastingly spoken by it. For it is not the case that one thing that was being said is finished and another is said so that all of them might be said; rather, all things are said at once and everlastingly. Otherwise, there would already be time and change and not true eternity nor true immortality.[54]

In what is eternal nothing ceases to be and nothing comes to be. "To the extent that anything is not what it was and is what it was not, to that extent it dies and is born. Nothing of your Word, then, passes away and comes to be, because it is truly immortal and eternal."[55] Contrasting eternity with time, Augustine says, "Nothing passes away in the eternal, but it is present as a whole. No time, however, is present as a whole."[56] Hence, God does not precede time by time:

> Otherwise you would not precede all times. But you precede all past times by the loftiness of ever present eternity, and you surpass all future times, because they are future, and when they come, they will be past. "But you are the Selfsame, and your years do not fail" (Ps 101:28). Your years neither come nor go. These years of ours come and go so that they may all come. All your years stand at once, because they stand still, and passing years are not shoved aside by those that come, because your years do not pass away. All these years of ours will be, when they will be no more. Your years are one day, and your day is not each day, but today, because your today does not give way to tomorrow or take the place of yesterday. Your today is eternity.[57]

One of Augustine's favorite names for God is "The Selfsame."[58] He says to God, "You are not one thing at one time and different at another, but the Selfsame, and the Selfsame, and the Selfsame...."[59] In commenting on Psalm 100, he claims that God's eternity is his very substance. "In it there is nothing past, as if it were no longer; there is nothing future, as if it were not yet. In it there is only 'Is'; there is in it no 'Was' and 'Will be,' because what was is no longer and what will be is not yet, but whatever is in it is only 'Is.'"[60]

Where did Augustine derive this concept of divine eternity as timeless all-at-onceness? Boethius

(480-525/6), who lived roughly a century after Augustine, is rightly credited with having passed on to the later Middle Ages this concept of divine eternity as life all at once. He expressed the idea in his well-known definition: "the perfect possession all at once of unending life."[61] All the elements of that definition are clearly found in Augustine, but before the time of Augustine that concept of eternity is found in no Christian thinker, except perhaps Gregory of Nyssa, who is more Augustine's contemporary than his source.[62]

Origen, the third-century Alexandrian theologian, provides an interesting example of a thinker who lacked the concept of divine eternity as distinct from time. Though Richard Sorabji finds in Origen, who was a contemporary of Plotinus, non-temporal senses for such terms as "was," "origin," and "always," he admits that Origen does not "always have a very firm grasp of the idea of timelessness."[63] In fact, Origen explicitly defined "the everlasting or eternal in the proper sense" as "that which did not have a beginning of its existence and can never cease to be what it is."[64] In their notes to this text, Henri Crouzel and Manlio Simonetti say that Origen came closer to a grasp of eternity as without succession in his *Homilies on Jeremiah* IX, 4, but add, "He does not seem to have come to a notion of eternity that clearly removed all succession."[65]

Like Augustine, Origen confronted the problem of God's idleness before creation. He claimed that it is "absurd and at the same time impious to suppose that God's powers [of creating and exercising providence] were at some point even for a moment idle." He adds, "For this reason one cannot suppose that there was even a single moment at which that beneficent power did not produce good.... And in this way it is seen to follow that there never was a moment where God was not creator, beneficent, and provident."[66] The absurdity and impiety, in other words, of supposing that God's powers were ever idle leads Origen to maintain that creatures always existed.[67] He concedes the difficulty of grasping how "creatures have always existed by reason of the fact that God is and that they subsisted, so to speak, without beginning, though we must believe without any doubt that they were created and made by God."[68] He very tentatively proposes a solution which occurs to him as avoiding all danger to piety: God the Father always existed and always had his only-begotten Son who is also called wisdom. "In this wisdom, which was always with the Father, creation was always present as described and formed, and there never was a moment when the prefiguration of those things which were to come was not present in that wisdom."[69] Crouzel and Simonetti comment, "The creation coeternal with God is the Intelligible World which contains the plans of creation and the seeds of the beings to come and is identified with the Son insofar as he is wisdom."[70] Lacking a concept of God's eternity as timeless, Origen could not avoid the problem of divine idleness in the way that Augustine did; rather, he had

to suppose an eternal creation in the wisdom of
God.[71] Though Sorabji finds some earlier traces of a
timeless eternity in Plutarch, Clement of Alexan-
dria, and Philo Judaeus, one must admit, as he does,
that "these authors do not always have a very firm
grasp on the idea of timelessness."[72]

Plotinus (205-269/270 A.D.), on the other hand,
clearly taught a doctrine of eternity as timelessness.
Because, however, the great Neoplatonist repeatedly
appealed to the authority of Parmenides and Plato,
historians of philosophy have at times taken his appeals to historical antecedents at their face value and
attributed to Parmenides and Plato the concept of
eternity as a complete absence of succession and duration. Denis O'Brien has argued convincingly that
such a concept of eternity is simply not to be found
prior to the *Enneads.*[73]

In *Ennead* III, 7, Plotinus speaks of eternity as an
endless life, all of which is present without either
past or future. He says,

> And if someone were in this way to speak of
> eternity as a life which is here and now endless
> because it is total and expends nothing of itself,
> since it has no past or future — for if it had, it
> would not now be a total life — he would be
> near to defining it.[74]

Again, commenting on Plato's words, "as eternity
remains in the one," he says that eternity is

the life, always the same, of real being around
the One; this, then, is what we are seeking; and
abiding like this is being eternity.... For true
being is never not being, or being otherwise;
and this is being always the same; and this is
being without any difference. So it does not
have any "this and that"; nor, therefore, will you
be able to separate it out or unroll it or prolong
it or stretch it; nor, then, can you apprehend
anything of it as before or after. If, then, there is
no before or after about it, but its "is" is the truest
thing about it, and itself, and this in the sense that
it is by its essence or life, then again there has come
to us what we are talking about, eternity.[75]

Unfortunately we do not have the Latin translation
of the *Enneads* by Marius Victorinus which Augustine read, but it is not difficult, I believe, to conjec-
ture what Victorinus's Latin must have been like and
to see Augustine's Latin reflecting the expressions of
Victorinus's translation.[76] In describing the nature
of the eternal, Plotinus says that

it is never other and is not a thinking or life that
goes from one thing to another but is always the
selfsame and without extension or interval; seeing all this one sees eternity in seeing a life that
abides in the same and always has the all present
to it, not now this, and then again that, but all
things at once, and not now some things, and
then again others, but a partless completion, as
if they were all together in a point, and had not
yet begun to go out and flow into lines; it is
something which abides in the same in itself and

> does not change at all but is always in the
> present, because nothing of it has passed away,
> nor again will anything of it come into being,
> but that which it is, it *is*....[77]

Hence, Augustine, it seems, was the first Christian
thinker, at least in the West, to have articulated the
philosophical concept of eternity as a life that is complete all at once in the present without any past or
future. In order to respond to the Manichaean question about what God was doing before he created
the world, he needed such a concept of divine eternity as timelessness, and he found that concept in
Plotinus, for there was simply nowhere else he could
have found it.

II. The Second Paradox

The resolution of our first paradox required a concept of eternity as having not merely no beginning
or end, but also no before or after, that is, as having
no temporal succession so that it is whole all at once.
Augustine next turns from the timeless eternity of
God to the temporal being of creatures. At no time
did God make nothing, since God made time itself,
and no times are coeternal with God, because, if
they lasted like eternity, they would not be times.
"What, then, is time?" Augustine asks. If no one
asks him, he knows what time is, but if he tries to
explain it to someone who asks, he does not know.[78]
He is, nonetheless, certain that if nothing passed

away, there would be no past time, that if nothing were coming, there would be no future time, and if nothing existed, there would be no present time.

1. The Search for an Extent of Time

Augustine's attempt to answer the question, "What is time?" is quickly transformed into a skeptical paradox, for neither past nor future time is, and present time *is* only by ceasing to be:

> How then do those two times, the past and the future, exist, if the past is no longer and the future is not yet? But if the present time were always present and did not move into the past, it would no longer be time, but eternity. If then the present, in order to be time, comes about precisely because it moves into the past, how can we say that it is, since the reason that it is is that it will not be. And so we can truly say that time is because it tends not to be.[79]

Given Augustine's quite Platonic way of thinking of God as the Selfsame, who alone truly is, because he is immutable and eternal, no creature can have true or genuine being. E. Gilson claimed that, because Augustine identified true being with the immutable self-sameness of God, he had no suitable term for the being of creatures except time.[80] That claim is not, I believe, quite correct, for Augustine certainly does insist that creatures are, though he also says that God alone truly is, since he is immutable.[81] The temporal character, nonetheless, of everything created indicates its radical contingency, its passing away, its very tendency not to be.[82]

The paradox is heightened. Augustine points out that we speak of a long time and a short time, when we are speaking of the past or future. But how, he asks, can what does not exist be either long or short? Since the past is no more, it cannot be long or short, and since the future is not yet, how can it be long or short? Worse yet, can the present be either long or short? We can speak of the present year, month, day, hour, or minute, but in each case what is past of each of them is no more and what is in the future is not yet. Hence, the present time contracts to a single moment.

> If we conceive a bit of time that cannot be divided into even the most minute parts of a moment, that alone is what may be called the present, but it, nonetheless, flies from the future into the past with such haste that it is not extended by the least amount.[83]

Hence, Augustine says, "The present has no extent."[84] The skeptical conclusion emerges: there is no time that can be long. "Present time cries out that it cannot be long."[85] But the immediately present moment cannot have even a short extent, since it has no extent. It is a passing instant, a point without extent.[86]

Augustine is convinced that we do, nonetheless, perceive extents of time and that we compare them and say that some are longer than others. "It is passing times that we measure, when we measure them by perceiving them. But who can measure past times which are no more or future times which are not yet, unless someone should dare to say that what is not can be measured?"[87] History and prophecy, moreover, presuppose that past and future have some being. "Those who tell of past events would surely not tell the truth, if they did not see those events with the mind. But if those events had no being, they could not be seen at all. Hence, past and future events have being."[88] Past and future, then, are somewhere, but wherever they are, they exist only as present. The things themselves have passed away. When one gives a true account of the past, "it is not the things themselves that are drawn from memory, but words conceived from their images which were implanted in the mind like footsteps as they passed through the senses."[89] So too, when future things are foreseen, "it is not the things themselves, which do not exist, that is, the things to come, but their causes, or perhaps signs of them, which already exist, that are seen."[90] Hence, Augustine again turns to prayer — a sure sign that the going has become difficult. He insists that it is now plain and clear that neither the past nor the future exist and that it is not correct to say that there are three times: past, present, and future. He suggests that we might say that there is the present of past things in memory, the present of present things in intuition, and the present of future things in expectation.[91] Yet he concedes that, as long as we understand that the past and the future are not now existing, we can say in accord with ordinary usage that there are these three times.[92] Augustine has, then, located the three times in the mind in present memory, intuition, and expectation. The present, however, is still the instant through which the future moves into the past so that there is no stretch of time to measure.

Augustine has claimed that we do measure passing times and that we know that we do. How does he know this? He answers, "I know this because we make such measurements, and we cannot measure things that do not exist, and neither past nor future things exist."[93] But the problem recurs: "How do we measure present time, since it has no extent?"[94] Time is measured as it passes from the future which does not yet exist through the present which has no extent into the past which is no more. Where then is there an extent which we measure when we measure passing times?

> In the future out of which it passes? But we do not measure what does not yet exist. Or in the present by which it passes? We do not measure what is without extent. Or in the past into which it passes? We do not measure what no longer is.[95]

Again Augustine turns to God in prayer, pleading that God grant him what he longs for, since God has given him this longing.[96]

He examines the claim of a learned man that the movements of the sun, moon, and stars constitute time.[97] But the movements of any one of these bodies cannot constitute time, since, even if one of them stopped moving, time would still go on. He points to the biblical account of the battle at Gibeon during which the sun stopped its movement, while time continued on, as confirmation that time is not constituted by the movement of any heavenly body.[98] From consideration of this battle he draws the tentative conclusion, "I see then that time is a certain distention. But do I see this? Or do only I think I see this? You will show me, O light, O truth!"[99]

Augustine rejects the idea that time is the movement of a body, for, though a body moves in time, it is not clear that the movement of a body constitutes time. Rather, he says that the movement of a body is distinct from that by which we measure how long the movement takes — and the latter is better called time.[100] Furthermore, we measure not merely the length of time that a body moves, but also the length of time it remains at rest; hence, time is not the movement of a body.[101]

Again in prayer Augustine asks whether he does not confess truly that he measures extents of time and answers, "Yes, O Lord, my God, I measure them and I know not what I measure. I measure the motion of a body in time. But do I not measure time itself?"[102] He asks whether he could measure the length of time of a body's movement unless he could measure the time in which the body is moved. He measures a longer time by a shorter time, for example, the length of a poem by the length of the verses, the length of the verses by the length of the feet, the length of the feet by the length of the syl-

lables as they sound. And yet this is not a reliable
measure of time, since one can pronounce a shorter
verse more slowly. Then he adds, in what seems to
be a definition of time: "For this reason it seemed to
me that time is nothing more than a distention. But of
what thing? That I do not know, but I would be sur-
prised if it is not a distention of the mind itself."[103]

2. Time as a Distention of the Mind

Twice Augustine has called time a distention.
What does he mean by "distention"? The Latin
distentio is a medical term that refers to a condition
of the body and bears a decidedly negative connotation. The *Oxford Latin Dictionary* gives: "access
of tension, spasm, distortion." The adjective *distentus*
means "swollen" or "distended." The root appears
in various other Latin verbs: *tendo, attendo, extendo,*
and *intendo,* from which we get the English verbs:
tend, attend, extend, and intend, as well as the cor-
responding nouns and adjectives. The prefix *dis-* in
distentio, and in many other compounds, has a negative connotation. While "attention" or "intention"
are good or neutral, "distention" is clearly negative.

This negative connotation of "distention" is explicitly found in Augustine's usage as well. In Book
Eight, he asks whether "diverse pleasures do not dis-
tend the human heart," where Henry Chadwick
translates the verb as "pull apart" and William Watts
has "rack."[104] There is also a parallel between the
distention of time and the extension of bodies.[105]

As a body swells in three dimensions, time swells out in a fourth dimension.[106] Augustine refers to the three-dimensional swelling of a body by the Latin term *tumor*,[107] which has the same negative connotation in Augustine's Latin as it does in English.[108] So too, the stretching out of time has the negative term *distentio*. This is quite Neoplatonic, and that, of course, should be no surprise, since Augustine's definition of time as a distention of the mind is surely derived from Plotinus.[109]

In the final chapters of Book Eleven the negative sense of "distention" emerges in language that is both Plotinian and Pauline. Augustine prays to his God, "See, my life is a distention, and your right hand has raised me up in my Lord, the Son of Man, the mediator between you the One and us the many who are dissipated on many things through many things...."[110] He prays that by following the One he "may be bound together" — perhaps "bandaged up" would be better — "from my old days — having forgotten the past, not distended to those things which are to come and will pass away, but extended to those thing which are before."[111] He adds that he pursues the reward of his "calling from above, not in distention, but with intention, where I may hear the voice of praise and contemplate your delight which neither comes nor passes."[112] Here the state of distention is a state of being pulled apart into manyness away from God, the One, to whom we are being called and pulled back. Augustine complains that his years are filled with groans, though

God, his eternal Father, is his consolation. He concludes with words which, taken literally, indicate his descent or fall into time.

> But I have leapt apart into times whose order I did not know, and my thoughts, the inmost parts of my soul, are ripped apart by tumultuous changes, until I flow together into you, purified and melted by the fire of your love.[113]

The distendedness that is our temporal condition is not merely the being of creatures; it is also our condition of being separated or having fallen away from the One.[114] Our being in time, it seems, is a penalty for sin.

In *De vera religione* Augustine says, "We have come down into temporal things, and by love of them we are kept from eternal things."[115] In the same work he compares the passing beauty of the whole temporal order to that of a song, arguing that it is just as unreasonable to want temporal things not to pass away as to want the individual notes of a song not to pass away, but to sound forever. He admits, nonetheless, that no human mind can see the whole temporal order as we can hear the whole of a song, and adds, "There is also the fact that we are not parts of the song, but we have become parts of the ages as a result of our condemnation."[116] And so, though "places offer us things to love, times steal from us what we love."[117] Worse yet, as parts of the ages, we too pass away.

> From early infancy to old age is a short space....
> No one brings yesterday back; tomorrow presses
> today to pass.... And right now while we are
> speaking, we are, of course, passing. Words run;
> hours fly; so our age, so our acts, so our honors,
> so our wretchedness, so this happiness of ours.
> All passes.[118]

In the *Confessions* Augustine speaks of himself as
having "flowed down" from his God, "having strayed
from God's stability," and having become "a land of
neediness."[119] The image of "our having flowed
down" is found in an early letter in which Augustine speaks of the past vision of intelligible things
seen by the mind and says that, "because we have
flowed down from them and begun to see other
things in another way, we see those former things
by reminiscence, that is by memory."[120] As we have
flowed down from the One, so "through continence
we are being pulled together and led back to the
One."[121] We are not alone in this situation, for "the
angel flowed down; the human soul flowed down,
and they revealed the abyss of the whole spiritual
creation."[122] Since our presence in time is the penalty of our fall, Augustine sees the purpose of Christ's
coming as to set us free from time. "Then, when
the fullness of time came, he came to set us free
from time."[123] And the result of his coming will be
that, "once we have been set free from time, we will
come to that eternity, where there is no time...."[124]
Hence, the distention that is time is not merely the
being of creatures; it is for us at least the penalty of

sin from which Christ has come to set us free. We
are, however, still left with our paradox: we measure
extents of time, but there seems to be no extent of
time to measure.

3. The Solution of the Paradox

We have already seen that Augustine derived from
Plotinus's *Ennead* III, 7 his concept of eternity as
the succession-less, ever-abiding present. Moreover,
we have seen that he contrasted time with such always abiding and present eternity. Hence, it should
come as no surprise that Augustine draws his definition of time from Plotinus as well. In *Ennead* III,
7, 11, Plotinus describes how time originated from
eternity and concludes,

> So the spreading out of life involves time; life's
> continual progress involves continuity of time,
> and life which is past involves past time. So
> would it be sense to say that time is the life of
> soul in a movement of passage from one way of
> life to another? Yes, for if eternity is life at rest,
> unchanging and identical and already un-
> bounded, and time must exist as an image of
> eternity…then we must say that there is, instead
> of life There, another life….[125]

Augustine's "*distentio animi*" clearly echoes Plotinus's
διάστασις ζωῆς. As Augustine contrasts the immutability of eternity with the constant change of
time, so Plotinus contrasts "the sameness and self-

identity and abiding" state of eternity with "that which does not abide in the same [state] but does one act after another," and "that which is not distended but [is] one" with "the image of the one, found in continuity."[126] In an earlier work Augustine had followed Plotinus and Plato in calling time the sign or vestige of eternity, though that designation is not found in the *Confessions*.[127] In the *Confessions* the emphasis is entirely on the contrast between eternity and time.

The second paradox still remains: Where is there something to measure? Augustine insists that he knows that he measures time. "Yet I do not measure the future, because it does not exist; I do not measure the present, because it is not stretched out in any extent; I do not measure the past, because it no longer exists. What then do I measure? Times that are passing, not times that are past. That is what I have said."[128] His problem is not that he lacks the know-how or technique for measuring times, but that he cannot find an extent of time that he can measure.[129] He knows that he does measure time, but there does not seem that there can be any extent of time to measure.

He appeals to the example of a voice that sounds. It cannot be measured after it has sounded or before it sounds; at the time it was sounding it could be measured, because at that time it existed. "While passing away it was being extended into some extent of time by which it could be measured, for the

present has no extent."[130] But where is this extent
that can be measured? Augustine is clear that he does
not measure the syllables themselves which have
ceased to exist; rather, he measures something that
remains fixed in his memory. Hence, he concludes,

> It is in you, my mind, that I measure times....
> It is in you, I say, that I measure extents of time.
> I measure the present impression that passing
> things make upon you and that remains, when
> those things have passed, and not the things
> which passed to produce it.[131]

The present impression made upon the mind by
passing things remains (*manet*). In the next para-
graph he insists that the mind's attention lasts
(*perdurat*). He argues,

> Who then would deny that future things are not
> yet? But there is, nonetheless, an expectation of
> future things in the mind. And who would deny
> that past things are not now? But there is,
> nonetheless, memory of past things in the mind.
> And who would deny that present time lacks
> extent, because it passes in a point? But atten-
> tion, nonetheless, endures, and through it what
> will be present continues to pass away.[132]

What is going on here? Some read Augustine as if
his final word on the present is that it has no extent.
In commenting on Augustine's claim that time is
"some kind of distention," Callahan says that,
though it fits the conviction that time is measured

as it passes, "there is still the difficulty that the only time that exists is an indivisible present."[133] Again he says, "The present, to be sure, is without extension…."[134] If Augustine's final word were that the present moment is an unextended point, then there would simply be no extent of time to be measured. Despite his statement that the present has no extent and is a point, Augustine insists that we do measure times, and it is a condition of anyone's being able to measure time that it have some extent. Here the impression which passing things make upon the mind remains, and the mind's attention endures. Many scholars overlook the significance of what Augustine says here. R. Jordan, for example, mentions that it is not immediately clear why time should be an extension of the mind rather than of something else.[135] The reason, I maintain, is that by its memory of the past, attention to the present, and expectation of the future the human mind is itself extended or distended in a way that beings that are not minds are not and cannot be extended. Augustine illustrates this point by the recitation of part of Ambrose's hymn, "*Deus creator omnium*: God, creator of all things." He means, I believe, that, if our attention were not extended, but instantaneous, we would hear only the syllable sounding at the present instant and would, then, never grasp whole words, or verses, or sentences. In order to grasp any meaning in the sounds of the verse we have to hold on to what has just sounded while we hear the present

sound and look forward to the coming sound, and
we have to synthesize the sequence of these sounds
which we hold before our mind's attention. That attention endures, and by its enduring it produces the
extendedness or distention of the mind which is time
and is a necessary condition for our perceiving any temporal object, such as the verse of Ambrose's hymn.

Augustine begins with the fact that we do perceive and measure stretches of time, and in Kantian
fashion he is looking for the conditions of our being able to do so. Immanuel Kant did something
similar with his account of the perception of a thing.
He maintained that to perceive a thing or an event
one needs many observations and one has to think
of what one has observed in those successive observations as belonging to a unity either all at once in
the case of a thing or successively in the case of an
event.[136] If one thought of the contents of many observations as unconnected, as not belonging to any
unity, one would never have the idea of a thing or
of an event. So too, Augustine is pointing toward
the conditions of the possibility of observing a temporal whole. If in hearing the syllables, *De-* and *us*
and *cre-* and *at-* and *or* and *om-* and *ni-* and *um*, we
did not hold the impression they make upon our
minds before our attention and synthesize them,
adding them together to form a temporal whole,
we could not grasp the meaning of the whole words
or of the whole verse. But in holding them before the
mind, the mind itself is stretched out, and that disten-

tion of the mind is an extent of time which provides us with something that can be measured. In his book on Augustine, *Was Ist Zeit?*, Kurt Flasch comments on the phrase: "*Attentio perdurat*: attention endures." He says,

> [Attention] holds fast the image of the passing objects over a stretch of time; it brings the remembered together with the expected in the present; it joins what was previously present with the now present. This makes up the extendedness of the time-producing soul, which does not live its life in a uniform instant, but successively.[137]

When we hear a verse, such as, "*Deus creator omnium*," from Ambrose's hymn, if our attention were not extended so that we held present before our mind the syllables that had already passed and anticipated those that would follow, we would be aware of only the presently sounding syllable. Augustine, it seems to me, implies that our present awareness must be extended or distended beyond the instantaneous present as a condition of our perceiving a temporal whole. That is, the temporal distention of the soul or mind is a necessary condition of our perceiving temporal wholes. Hence, the second paradox about time is resolved through coming to see that the distention of mind or soul is a necessary condition of our perceiving temporal sequences. The mind or soul is itself distended in the action of reciting a song, and the distended bits make up the whole of one's life. In Augustine's words,

The life of this action of mine is distended into
memory by reason of that part I have spoken
and into forethought by reason of the part I am
about to speak. But attention is actually present
and that which was to be is borne along by it so
as to become past…. The same thing holds for
a longer action, of which the Psalm is a small
part. The same thing holds for a man's entire
life, the parts of which are all the man's actions.
The same thing holds throughout the whole
ages of the sons of men, the parts of which are
the lives of all men.[138]

Hence, Augustine resolves the second paradox and
finds an extent of time in the mind's distention. The
key to the solution, if not all its elements, is found
in the Plotinian definition of time as διάστασις
ζωῆς. This way of resolving the paradox may strike
one as quite unsatisfactory. And that unsatisfactori-
ness takes us to the final paradox.

III. The Third Paradox

We have seen that Augustine defines — or at least
seems to define — time as a distention and as a distention of the mind. In examining the previous paradox I have tried to illustrate how, though the past is
no more and the future is not yet, and though the
present is the unextended point through which the
future moves into the past, the present, nonetheless, acquires an extent insofar as the human mind
is distended through remembering the immediate

past and anticipating the oncoming future. However, if the perdurance of present attention provides an extent or stretch of time that can be measured, the distention that for Augustine constitutes time is a distention of the mind, and that brings us to the final paradox or problem of this lecture. If time is such a distention of the mind, does it not follow that Augustine's account of time is really quite preposterous?

1. The Objection to Augustine's Account

Perhaps the clearest statement of this objection to Augustine's definition of time was formulated by Bertrand Russell. Great logician though he was, Russell nicely illustrates the informal fallacy called "poisoning the well," when he blames Augustine's "absorption in the sense of sin" for having "led him to excessive subjectivity" so that he "was content to substitute subjective time for the time of history and physics." He adds that for Augustine,

> Memory, perception, and expectation…made up all that there is of time. But obviously this won't do. All his memories and all his expectations occurred at about the time of the fall of Rome, whereas mine occur at about the time of the fall of industrial civilization, which formed no part of the bishop of Hippo's expectations. Subjective time might suffice for a solipsist of the moment, but not for a man who believes in a real past and future, even if only his own.[139]

As Russell understood him, Augustine simply re-
placed the common and public time of history and
physics with the private and subjective time of each
individual's mind. On Russell's interpretation, time
is a distention or extension of individual human
minds, and from such a position it would follow
that there simply could be no time before human
minds — or perhaps other rational minds — existed. The problem is not merely that scientific evidence indicates that human beings were relative late-
comers into this world and that, if time is the distention of individual human minds, there could have
been no time before human beings existed.[140] The
more serious problem is that, according to Russell's
reading of Augustine, each of us would have our
own private psychological time — the sort of time
which passes more quickly when we are having fun,
but much more slowly when we are doing something unpleasant or uninteresting — and that would
be the only time there is.[141] If time were merely such
a private content of individual minds, there would
be no public time common to us all. If that were the
case, it would be quite impossible for many of us to
agree upon a time, as we did in gathering here this
afternoon, that is common and public to all of us.

If Augustine had nothing else to say about time
than what he said in Book Eleven of the *Confessions*, we might be left with this highly subjective
account of time and be forced to agree with Russell's
conclusion, "Obviously this won't do." The situa-

tion is bettered — or perhaps worsened — depend-
ing on how you view the choice between idealism
or inconsistency by what Augustine says elsewhere.
In the *City of God*, Augustine explicitly states, "Time
existed when there was no human being."[142] That could
not be the case if time had for Augustine the subjective
sort of being that Russell claimed it had, unless, of
course, Augustine was inconsistent or simply changed
his mind by the time he wrote the later work.

2. Some Solutions to the Problem

There are a number of ways in which students of
Augustine have tried to extricate him from what they
recognized as a highly subjective account of time.
Some have argued that in Book Eleven of the *Confessions* Augustine was not giving an account of time,
but of a certain kind of time, i.e., psychological time,
and that he obviously held that there was also another
sort of time. For example, in his article, "Augustine's
Two Theories of Time," John Morrison finds in Augustine a subjective theory of time in the *Confessions*
and an objective view of time in the *City of God*.[143]
Jean Guitton likewise finds in Augustine at least two
sorts of time which he refers to as "le temps de l'histoire
personelle" et "le temps de l'histoire intégrale."[144]

Did Augustine then change his mind about the
nature of time by the date of the *City of God*, substi-
tuting in his later work a public and objective sort
of time for the private and subjective time of the

Confessions? Against the supposition that he changed his mind after the *Confessions*, there are, however, texts prior to that work as well as others subsequent to it in which he clearly stated that time began with the creation of heaven and earth. For instance, in his earliest commentary on Genesis, *De Genesi contra Manichaeos*, written in 387 or 388, approximately ten years before the *Confessions*, he asked, "How, after all, was there a time which God had not made, since he is the maker of all time? And if time began with heaven and earth, a time cannot be found when God had not yet made heaven and earth."[145] So too, he said, "God, of course, made the world, and thus time began to be along with the creation that God made...."[146] Even in the *Confessions* Augustine clearly maintained that time began with the creation of heaven and earth, for in answer to the Manichaean question that asked what God was doing before he made heaven and earth, Augustine insisted, as we have seen, that before God created heaven and earth there was no time and, therefore, no time during which God did nothing.[147] In the *City of God*, Augustine clearly maintained, "Where, after all, there is no creature, by whose changing motions times are traversed, times cannot exist at all."[148] And in his *De Genesi ad litteram*, he said,

> Time began to run its course with the motions of creatures that God made; hence, it is pointless to look for time before creatures, as if one could find time before time. If there were no

motion of either a spiritual or bodily creature by which the future moves through the present into the past, there would be no time at all.[149]

Augustine, in fact, seems to offer a definition of time in this work when he says that time "is the motion of creatures from one state to another as things succeed one another in accord with the decree of God who governs all the things he has made."[150]

Hence, though there do not seem to be grounds for the claim that Augustine changed his view of time from the *Confessions* to the *City of God*, there are, it would seem, some grounds for holding that Augustine had at least two different concepts of time: the one, the subjective and private concept of time as the distention of the mind, and the other, the objective concept of time as the motion of creatures by which they succeed one another.

One way of resolving the sort of objection raised by Russell against Augustine's account of time, then, maintains that Augustine had two accounts of time. In Book Eleven of the *Confessions* Augustine presented an account of subjective or psychological time, i.e., as the distention of the mind, while he elsewhere gave an account of objective or physical time, i.e., as the motion of creatures that began with the creation of heaven and earth.

Another way of resolving the puzzle or paradox that we have been examining is to maintain that in Book Eleven of the *Confessions* Augustine is not concerned with a definition of time or an account of the nature of time, but is presenting an account of our experience of time. John Cavadini, for example, maintains that "Augustine is much more interested in analyzing our awareness of time as itself a phenomenon worthy of investigation, rather than in settling questions about time itself in a definitive way."[151] Other authors recognize that Augustine set out to find a definition of time, but maintain that he never came up with such a definition. Gerard O'Daly, for example, says, "Augustine suggests at the beginning of his discussion that he is inquiring into the nature of time itself," but O'Daly claims that "he does not give an answer to this question, or a *definition* of time, in the course of his investigation."[152] Henry Chadwick finds Augustine's discussion of time remarkably close to "the Sceptical or 'Academic' position that for the human mind the question is unanswerable." He adds, "At least Augustine does not answer it."[153]

As attractive and attractively simple as these solutions of the paradox, or ways of escaping the problem, may seem, they do not, I believe, have very solid textual support. We have already seen that in Book Eleven of the *Confessions* Augustine repeatedly asks, "What is time?" and says that he wants to know "the power and nature of time" — expressions which seem clearly to indicate that he was looking for a definition of time. Such questions also indicate that he was not looking for a definition of a particular sort of time, but of time *sans phrase*.[154] Furthermore, the discussion of the relation between eternity and time, for instance, in replying to the Manichaean objection about what God was doing before he made heaven and earth, presupposes that the time under discussion is not some sort of subjective or psychological time, but the time which is the being of creatures as opposed to the being of the creator. It would, after all, have been pointless for Augustine to respond to the Manichaean question with the claim that there was no psychological time before God created heaven and earth. Augustine says, moreover, that human life is a distention and that the state of the created mind is varied and its awareness distended by the expectation of what is to come and by memory of the past. But far different is God's being, knowing, and activity. Augustine confesses, "As you knew heaven and earth in the beginning without any variation of your knowledge, so you made heaven and earth in the beginning without any distention of your activity."[155] My point is that Augustine's contrasting the non-distendedness of God's being, knowing, and activity with the distendedness of a creature's being, knowing, and activity presupposes that he is contrasting eternity with time, not eternity with a kind of time.[156] Finally, as we have already seen in examining the first two paradoxes, Augustine developed his accounts of both eternity and time in dependence upon Plotinus's *Ennead* III, 7, and it is clear, I believe, that Plotinus was not presenting an account of one sort of time among several, but of time *simpliciter*.

3. A Plotinian Solution to the Problem

There is another solution to this paradox we have been examining. We have seen that the solution to the first and the second paradoxes were dependent upon Plotinus's treatment of eternity and time in *Ennead* III, 7. Without the concept of eternity free from all succession, Augustine could not have successfully dealt with the Manichaean question about what God was doing before he made heaven and earth. So too, without the Plotinian concept of time as a distention of the mind, Augustine could not have explained how we could have an extent of time to measure, something we all obviously do when we know that this time is longer than that. Hence, it should not seem implausible that the solution to the third paradox may also be found in Plotinus.

If we look at the section of *Ennead* III, 7, 11, immediately prior to the definition of time as διάστασις ζωῆς, we find that in describing the emergence of time from eternity, Plotinus is speaking of Soul with a capital S — of the universal soul. He says that the universal soul,

> making the world of sense in imitation of that other world, moving with a motion that is not that which exists There, but like it, and intending to be an image of it, first of all put itself into time, which it made instead of eternity, and then handed over that which came into being as a slave to time, by making the whole of it exist in time and encompassing all its ways with time.[157]

Furthermore, since the sensible world moves in Soul,
for "there is no other place of it (this universe) than
Soul, it moves also in the time of Soul."[158] Hence,
when Plotinus speaks of "the spreading out of life"
(διάστασις ζωῆς), he is primarily thinking of the
distention of the Soul which makes this whole sensible world. And that distention is obviously one,
public, and common to all.

Toward the end of *Ennead* III, 7, Plotinus spells
out, albeit somewhat cryptically, the relationship between this universal soul and individual souls. He
asks, "How, then, is time everywhere?" And he answers, "Because Soul, too, is not absent from any
part of the Universe, just as the soul in us is not
absent from any part of us."[159] He also asks, "Is time,
then, also in us?" His answer makes it clear that time
is in every human soul:

> It is in every soul of this kind, and in the same
> form in every one of them, and all are one. So
> time will not be split up any more than eternity,
> which, in a different way, is in all the [eternal
> beings] of the same form.[160]

Hence, when Plotinus defines time as διάστασις
ζωῆς — as a distention of life — he is speaking,
first of all, of the universal soul and only second-
arily of individual human souls which are in the
universal soul and which are one with that Soul. In
the words of Aimé Solignac, Plotinus "met le temps
dans l'Ame universelle et peut ainsi donner une sig-

nification au temps des choses."[161] For Plotinus there
is an objective *temps des choses* which is not frag-
mented into the subjective times of individual human souls, because all souls are one and because they
are in the universal soul whose διάστασις constitutes time. Hence, if one were to look for a solution
to Augustine's third paradox about time in Plotinus,
one would find that Plotinus's solution lies in the
universal soul which makes the world and provides
an objective time in which all individual human
souls exist. But can that solution have been
Augustine's?

Some years ago, in a paper on this question, I very
tentatively drew the conclusion

> that there is good reason for believing that as
> late as the time of his writing the *Confessions*,
> when he was already a Christian bishop, Augus-
> tine still held, if not as an explicit doctrine, at
> least as an implicit, but operative element of his
> conceptual scheme, the idea of a universal or
> world-soul with which individual souls are one,
> from which individual souls have fallen, and in
> virtue of which his definition of time as *'distentio
> animi'* can escape charges of inconsistency with
> what he says elsewhere about time as well as
> charges that such a definition of time is purely
> subjective and hopelessly idealistic. For, time, if
> my very tentatively suggested hypothesis is cor-
> rect, is for Augustine as it was for Plotinus
> primarily a distention of that soul by which
> form is given to the world and with which we are
> all somehow one.[162]

I have for some time wanted to return to that thesis which I now believe has better support than I had originally thought, at least in part because of the studies on time done by Kurt Flasch and Udo Jenk.[163]

4. The Universal Soul in Augustine

Obviously, if the Plotinian solution to the third paradox is to be found in Augustine, he must have held a doctrine of a universal soul of which individual human souls are in some sense parts. There are a number of texts in Augustine which make it quite clear that he did think, especially but not exclusively in his earlier writings, that there is such a universal soul. His comments on his earlier view in his *Retractationes* often cast even clearer light upon his thinking.

For instance, in one of his earliest works written at Cassiciacum, Augustine speaks of "that soul which is either in us or everywhere." He says, most probably with the Neoplatonists in mind, "Only the most exceptional kind of person is able to use [reason] as a guide to understand God or that soul which is either in us or everywhere, precisely because it is difficult for one who has plunged into the concerns of these senses to return to oneself."[164] In another early and very difficult work, Augustine speaks of a soul which animates the whole world:

> This order means that that highest essence gives
> form to body through soul, by which it [body]
> is to the extent that it is. Therefore, body
> subsists through soul, and it is by the very fact
> that it is animated, either universally, as the
> world, or particularly, as each animal within the
> world…. Nor is there found something that is
> between the highest life, which is immutable
> wisdom and truth, and that to which life is last
> given, i.e., body, except life-giving soul.[165]

Admittedly, Augustine did say of this passage in his
Retractationes, "All this was said with utter rash-
ness."[166] It seems, however, that the reason he found
this "rash" was that the view was supported neither
by certain argument nor by the scriptures. For, in
commenting on a passage in *De musica* in which he
had implied that this world is a living being, Augustine notes that, though Plato and others thought
that the world was ensouled, he has not been able
to settle this point by certain argument and finds
no solid support for it in the scriptures.[167] He says
that he called the view that there is a world-soul
rash, "not because I maintain that it is false, but
because I do not grasp that it is true that the world
is a living being."[168] He adds, "Even if the world is
not a living being, there is, nonetheless, a spiritual
and living power which serves God in his holy angels to adorn and administer the world. This is correctly believed even by those who do not understand it."[169] In any case, Augustine insists that, if

there is such a soul, it is not God, but a creature that God made.[170]

In his *De Genesi ad litteram liber imperfectus*, a text begun in 393 just a few years before he began his *Confessions*, Augustine offered as a possible meaning for the spirit that moved over the waters in Genesis 1:2:

> the living creature which contains and moves this visible universe and all bodies and to which God gave a certain power of serving him for working in those things which come to be. This spirit is better than every ethereal body, because every invisible creature has precedence over every visible creature; hence, it is not unreasonably called the spirit of God.[171]

In another text written at the time of the *Confessions*, Augustine expresses considerable hesitancy about the existence of a world-soul, though he certainly does not reject it.

> But whether this whole bodily mass, which is called the world, has some soul or something like a soul of its own, that is, rational life by which it is ruled like each animal, is a great and hidden question. This opinion should not be affirmed unless it is found to be true, nor should it be rejected unless it is found to be false.[172]

Hence, these texts on the world-soul or universal soul show that even in the last years of his life, Au-

gustine had not ruled out the possibility of such a
soul and could speak in the singular of "a spiritual
and living power" serving God "in his angels to
adorn and administer the world."

But how are our souls related to such a soul?
Augustine's remark in *De quantitate animae* where
he takes up the question about the number of souls
suggests an answer to this question. After first having tried to shelve the question as being too difficult, Augustine offers Evodius, his partner in the
dialogue, this odd answer:

> For if I tell you that there is one soul, you will be
> disturbed because in one person it is happy and
> in another unhappy, for one and the same thing
> cannot be both happy and unhappy at the same
> time. If I say that it is one and many at the same
> time, you will laugh, and I would not easily find
> a way to put a stop to your laughter. But if I say
> that souls are simply many, I shall have to laugh
> at myself, and I will endure less well my dissat-
> isfaction with myself than your dissatisfaction
> with me.[173]

Augustine clearly rejects the idea that there is just
one soul as well as the idea that there are simply
many souls. The implication is, of course, that soul
is both one and many or that individual souls are
somehow one with the universal soul, the very same
sort of idea that we found in Plotinus.[174] This text
unfortunately stands alone, I believe, in Augustine's
works as the only text in which he discusses the num-

ber of souls. Moreover, it lacks the full clarity that one would like. However, there is, I believe, further evidence which, if not conclusive, at least points in the same direction.

Augustine held a very Platonic view of the human person in accord with which the real "I" was the incorporeal soul. Given such a view, the question of what makes souls to be individual souls becomes an implicit problem. Augustine once suggested that soul can only be divided by reason of different bodies. In an early dialogue, he tells his friend Evodius that his mind needs training if he is to understand "whether what certain very learned men say is actually true: namely, that the soul can in no way be divided in itself, but that this is possible by reason of the body."[175] He even goes so far as to suggest that our souls are not in our bodies.[176] As non-bodily beings not confined to bodies, souls cannot be separated from each other spatially any more than our souls can be spatially separated from God. Augustine, for example, insists that we can be separated from God only by sin and that it is not by feet or distances of place, but by our loves that we depart from or return to God.[177] Hence, in writing to Nebridius, a friend whose ill health kept him in Carthage and away from Augustine in Thagaste, Augustine advises his friend to enter his mind and raise it to God. "For there you more certainly also have us — not through bodily images, which one must now use in our recollection, but through that

thought by which you know we are together non-
spatially."[178] And in another early work he maintains that "the union of the mind is greater than
that of places or times...."[179] In the *Confessions* he
seems to have taken Horace's description of his friend
as "half my soul: *dimidium animae meae*" in so literal a sense that he later found it embarrassing.[180]
And yet, he frequently, even in later life, seems to
take the description of the early Christian community as having one heart and one soul in a similarly
literal sense — so much so that he says, "If then,
when we think the same thing and love each other,
my soul and your soul become one soul, how much
more is God the Father and God the Son one God
in the source of love."[181] All of these texts, I suggest,
indicate that Augustine thought that souls are united
with other souls to become one soul very much in
the way Plotinus did.

Hence, the elements requisite for the Plotinian
solution to the third paradox are present in Augustine, since he held, even if with something less than
full clarity and certitude, a universal soul of which
all individual souls are in some sense parts or with
which they are one. There is a difference between
the two thinkers insofar as Plotinus begins with the
universal soul and moves to individual souls which
are somehow one with it, while Augustine clearly
begins with individual human souls and moves to a
universal mind or soul that embraces all of time,
when he says,

> Surely, if there is a mind possessed of such great
> knowledge and foreknowledge, so that to it are
> known all things past and future, just as I know
> one familiar Psalm, then truly amazing is that
> mind and a source of awe and fear. From it
> whatever there is of ages past and of ages to come
> is no more hidden than there are hidden from
> me as I sing that Psalm what and how much
> preceded from its beginning and what and how
> much remains to the end.[182]

Kurt Flasch says that the reader who earlier in the
text of Book Eleven found no need for the hypoth-
esis of the world-soul or who rejected it on the
grounds that the Christian theologian would certainly not employ such a pagan idea must hold that
Augustine is here speaking of God.[183] But such a
reader must then face Augustine's next words:
"Heaven forbid that you, creator of the universe,
creator of souls and bodies, heaven forbid that you
should know everything past and future in that way.
You know them in a way that is far, far more marvelous and far more hidden."[184] Hence, the mind
that Augustine mentions in *Confessions* XI, 31, 41
can only be the universal soul with which each individual soul is somehow one. For these reasons I believe that Augustine resolved that third paradox in
this very Plotinian fashion so that time is not the
distention merely of individual souls, but of the
universal soul of which individual souls are in some
sense parts.

IV. Conclusion

We have examined three paradoxes or problems concerning time in Book Eleven of the *Confessions*. First, in order to be able to maintain that there was no time before God created the world and to avoid in that way the idea of God's being idle — just "hanging out," as our young folk say, for endless ages — he needed a concept of timeless eternity. He was, I have argued, the first Christian thinker — at least the first in the West — to articulate with clarity the concept of divine eternity as timeless, as being all at once without past or future. I have argued, moreover, that he derived that concept from Plotinus's *Ennead* III, 7 — a concept not found prior to Plotinus or clearly expressed after him before the time of Augustine. Second, in his search for a definition or an account of time, Augustine was faced with the paradox that past time is no more, that future time is not yet, and that the present is an instant through which the future passes into the past. That paradox left him with no stretch or extent of time that he could measure. In his resolution of this paradox he exploited in a way that Plotinus did not the Plotinian definition of time as διάστασις ζωῆς. He claimed that the individual mind must be distended in order to understand the meaning of a temporal series of sounds, as in the recitation of a Psalm or singing of a hymn; and he showed how the present can have an extent, moving from individual minds to the "the whole age of the sons of men, the parts of which are the lives of men." Finally, we have seen that Augustine resolved the third paradox of time by holding that time is ultimately the distention of the universal soul or mind of which individual souls are parts, so that in Book Eleven of the *Confessions* Augustine does give a definition of time — time which is the distention of individual human souls, but which is also the distention of the universal soul. Hence, Augustine escapes Russell's objection in the same way that Plotinus did.

In the prenotes to this lecture I suggested that a close examination of the paradoxes of time in Book Eleven of the *Confessions* would cast light upon the question of the unity of the work. In view of the heavy Plotinian influence upon Augustine's understanding of eternity and of time that this lecture has pointed out, I find confirmation for the view that sees the *Confessions* not so much an autobiography with an appendix on the Hexaemeron, as an attempt to present a Christian and Plotinian understanding of human existence. The *Confessions* is not so much the autobiography of Augustine as it is the story of every human being, and that story is a Christian and at the same time a very Plotinian account of our origin and fall, our present pilgrimage away from our fatherland, and our return to the fatherland where the Father is.[185]

When I first proposed the view that Augustine's view of time as a distention of the mind presup-

posed as part of his conceptual scheme a world-soul
or universal soul with which individual souls are
somehow one, I was bothered by a problem which I
expressed as follows: "If the world-soul is distended
in the creation of the world, is not the soul's fall
into time the same as the creation of the world? Or,
in Christian terms, do not creation and original sin
coincide?"[186] I no longer see the problem quite so
sharply. It would take more time and space than the
confines of this lecture permit to clarify this problem. But I think the solution can be found in Book
Twelve where Augustine speaks of our once being
part of the heaven of heavens and of our sharing in
God's eternity from which we have fallen into time.
For though time may have come into being with
the creation of the world, we rational souls were
meant to remain in contemplation of God as par-
takers of his eternity.[187]

   In conclusion, one might object that all this talk
of a world-soul or universal soul in Augustine, even
if it is there and resolves the third paradox, has no
relevance to contemporary philosophy or theology.
Augustine has, however, whether one likes it or not,
formed the way the Christian West thinks and speaks
about God and human existence. For example, the
idea of our individual souls or minds being somehow one with the universal soul is reflected in
Augustine's way of thinking of our relationship to
Adam. He says, "We, after all, were all in that one
man, when we were all that one man who fell into

sin through the woman who was made from him before the sin."[188] In speaking of our relation to Adam according to Augustine, John Rist says,

> The relationship between Adam and each of us looks in some respects like that of the Plotinian hypostasis of Soul...to the individuals which are 'parts' of it.... It is no more surprising that Adam can also exist 'separately' from his 'parts' than that the Plotinian hypostasis can exist 'apart' from individual souls; as a 'one and many.' The difference is that while Plotinus makes the individual souls metaphysically distinct from the hypostasis, Augustine makes them 'historically' distinct. But that is what we should expect a Christianized Plotinus to do.[189]

If, then, the Plotinian universal soul underlies the way Augustine conceived our relationship to Adam so that he could say, "We were all that one man," does it not follow that the Plotinian Soul also has something to do with the way he conceived our relationship to the Second Adam in his doctrine of the whole Christ: *integer Christus*? For, as Augustine insisted in his classic work against the heresy of Pelagius, *De gratia Christi et de peccato originali*, "In the impact of these two men the Christian faith properly consists."[190]

Notes

1. *Confessiones* XI, 14, 17: CCL 27, 202: "Quid est ergo tempus? Si nemo ex me quaerat, scio; si quaerenti explicare uelim, nescio...."

2. *Ibid.* XI, 23, 30: CCL 27, 209: "Ego scire cupio uim naturamque temporis...." That Augustine intended to define time is a disputed point which will be discussed in the third part of this talk. Translations from the *Confessions* are based on *The Confessions of St. Augustine*, tr. John K. Ryan (Garden City, NY: Image Books, 1960), though I have at times made changes in Ryan's translation; translations of other works of Augustine are my own.

3. In *Saint Augustin et la fin de la culture antique* (Paris: de Boccard, 1938), p. 61, Henri-Irénée Marrou ventured to say, "Augustin compose mal." But he took back that statement in the second volume of that work (Paris: de Boccard, 1949), pp. 665-72. For an excellent introduction to recent interpretations of the *Confessions*, see James J. O'Donnell's *Augustine: Confessions.* vol. I. *Introduction and Text* (Oxford: Clarendon Press, 1992), pp. xvii-li. Also see the introduction to Robert J. O'Connell's *St. Augustine's Confessions: The Odyssey of Soul* (Cambridge, MA: Belknap Press, 1969), pp. 1-22, for a presentation of the problem of the unity of the work. O'Connell's book offers a solution to that problem which I find right on target.

4. For Augustine's principles of scriptural exegesis, see my
"Criteria for Figurative Interpretation in St. Augustine," in *De Doctrina Christiana: A Classic of Western
Culture*, ed. Duane W. H. Arnold and Pamela Bright
(Notre Dame: University of Notre Dame Press, 1995),
pp. 109-22. Some editors of the *Confessions* appar-
ently regard the work as basically autobiographical,
for they omit the last three or four books as if they were
unnecessary. Sheed and Ward, for example, published
only the first ten books of F. J. Sheed's translation in
1942; Prentice-Hall published selections of the Latin
text from the first nine books in 1931, and in 1987
Aschendorff also published Latin selections with German commentary from the first ten books. If, however, the *Confessions* is a work of art, such a truncation
is analogous to dropping the last act of *Hamlet*.

5. It is commonly recognized that Augustine read at least
some of the *Enneads* of Plotinus in the months immediately preceding his baptism. Scholars are still divided about how many of the *Enneads* Augustine read
at this early period, about whether he already at this
time read some of Porphyry, and about which of the
two Neoplatonists had the greater influence upon
him. See my "St. Augustine's Use of 'Manens in Se,'"
Revue des études augustiniennes 32 (1993), 304-05,
note 65, for a list of *Enneads* that Augustine read or
probably read. See the articles by Frederick Van Fleteren
and R. J. O'Connell in *Augustinian Studies* 21 (1990),
83-152, for the current state of the question.

6. John M. Rist, *Augustine: Ancient Thought Baptized* (Cambridge: Cambridge Univ. Press, 1994), pp. 19-20.

7. *Ibid.*, p. 7.

8. Hans Urs von Balthasar, *Die Bekenntnisse* (Einsiedeln, 1985), p. 29: "Die Confessiones sind Gebet, Zwiesprache im Chor der mitbetenden Gemeinschaft; wen sie zum Mitbeten bewegen, der hat das Wesentliche an ihnen verstanden." The translation is mine; I owe the reference to Kurt Flasch, *Was Ist Zeit? Augustinus von Hippo. Das XI. Buch der Confessiones. Historisch-Philosophische Studie. Text – Übersetzung – Kommentar* (Frankfurt am Main: Klostermann, 1993), p. 206.

9. A quick search of Book Eleven turns up abundant examples of such prayer for understanding. For example, *Confessiones* XI, 3, 5: CCL 27, 196 and 197: "Audiam et intellegam, quomodo in principio fecisti caelum et terram…. Cum ergo illum interrogare non possim, te, quo plenus uera dixit, ueritas, rogo, te, deus meus, rogo, parce peccatis meis, et qui illi seruo tuo dedisti haec dicere, da et mihi haec intellegere"; and XI, 30, 40: CCL 27, 215: "Extendantur etiam in ea, quae ante sunt, et intellegant te ante omnia tempora aeternum creatorem omnium temporum neque ulla tempora tibi esse coaeterna nec ullam creaturam, etiamsi est aliqua supra tempora."

10. On this theme, see T. J. Van Bavel, "L'humanité du Christ comme *lac parvulorum* et comme *via* dans la spiritualité de saint Augustin," *Augustiniana* 7 (1957), 245-81. In the closing prayer of Book Eleven Augustine clearly distinguishes between believers who have attained understanding and those who have not. *Confessiones* XI, 31, 41: CCL 27, 215: "Qui intellegit,

confiteatur tibi, et qui non intellegit, confiteatur tibi."
See *In Iohannis evangelium tractatus* 98, 6: CCL 36,
579: "Proinde nec sic paruuli sunt lactandi, ut semper
non intelligant Deum Christum: nec sic ablactandi, ut
deserant hominem Christum."

11. *Epistula* 120, 1, 2: CESL 34/2: 705-06: "ueritatem ex
fide magis quam ex ratione percipi oportere; si enim
fides, inquis, sanctae ecclesiae ex disputationis ratione
et non ex credulitatis pietate adprehenderetur, nemo
praeter philosophos atque oratores beatitudinem
possideret."

12. See *ibid.* 120, 3, 13: CSEL 34/2, 716: "Intellectum
uero ualde ama."

13. *Retractationes* II, 6, 1: BA 12, 460: "Confessionum
mearum libri tredecim et de malis et de bonis meis
Deum laudant iustum et bonum, atque in eum exci-
tant humanum intellectum et affectum. Interim quod
ad me attinet, hoc in me egerunt cum scriberentur et
agunt cum leguntur. Quid de illis alii sentiant, ipsi
uiderint; multis tamen fratribus eos multum placuisse
et placere scio."

14. Though some contemporaries seem to isolate the
spiritual and the intellectual life, Augustine certainly
did not do that. In fact, as I have argued in a series of
articles, when he spoke of the spiritual person (*homo
spiritualis*), he meant not merely a Christian believer,
but someone who had risen to a Plotinian understanding of the faith. See my "'Homo spiritualis' in the
Confessions of St. Augustine," in *Augustine: From*

Rhetor to Theologian (Waterloo, Ontario: Wilfred Laurier Univ. Press, 1992), pp. 67-76; "Spirituals and Spiritual Sense in St. Augustine," *Augustinian Studies* 15 (1984), 65-81; "*Homo spiritalis* in St. Augustine's *De Genesi contra Manichaeos*," *Studia Patristica* 10, vol. 22, pp. 351-55.

15. See *Confessiones* I, 2, 2: CCL 27, 1-2: "Et quomodo inuocabo deum meum, deum et dominum meum, quoniam utique in me ipsum eum uocabo, cum inuocabo eum? … Quoniam itaque et ego sum, quid peto, ut uenias in me, qui non essem, nisi esses in me?"

16. *Ennead* V, 1, 6, ll. 9-12: ὧδε οὖν λεγέσθω θεὸν αὐτὸν ἐπικαλεσαμένοις οὐ λόγῳ γεγονῷ, ἀλλὰ τῇ ψυχῇ ἐκτείνασιν ἑαυτοὺς εἰς εὐχὴν πρὸς ἐκεῖνον, εὔχεσθαι τοῦτον τὸν τρόπον δυναμένους μόνους πρὸς μόνον. The Greek text of the *Enneads* along with the English translation throughout this volume is taken from *Plotinus*, with an English translation by A. H. Armstrong in seven volumes (Cambridge: Harvard Univ. Press, 1966-1988); here V, pp. 28-29.

17. Peter Brown, *Augustine of Hippo: A Biography* (Berkeley: University of California Press, 1967), p. 166.

18. *Ibid.*, p. 167, where Brown quotes from E. R. Dodds, "Augustine's Confessions: A Study of Spiritual Maladjustment," *Hibbert Journal* 26 (1927-28), 459-73, here 471 (cited from Brown).

19. During the recent past much has been written on the subject of time in St. Augustine. Book-length studies

include: Jean Guitton, *Le temps et l'éternité chez Plotin et saint Augustin*, 3rd ed. (Paris: J. Vrin, 1959); E. P. Meijering, *Augustin über Schöpfung, Ewigkeit und Zeit: Das elfte Buch der Bekenntnisse* (Leiden: Brill, 1979); and Kurt Flasch, *Was Ist Zeit?* Also see my articles: "The World-Soul and Time in St. Augustine," *Augustinian Studies* 14 (1983), 75-92, and "*Vocans Temporales, Faciens Aeternos*: St. Augustine on Liberation from Time," *Traditio* 41 (1985), 29-47, as well as John Cavadini, "Time and Ascent in *Confessiones* XI," in *Augustine: Presbyter Factus Sum*, ed. J. Lienhard, E. Muller, and R. Teske (New York: Peter Lang, 1994), pp. 171-85.

20. In *Epistula* 224 2: CSEL 57, 453, to Quodvultdeus, deacon of the church of Carthage, Augustine mentions that he has completed two volumes of his *Retractationes* in which he reviewed his two hundred and thirty-two books and that he still has his letters and homilies to do. To arrive at the number two hundred and thirty-two, Augustine counted books (*libri*) in the sense in which one work (*opus*), such as the *Confessions* contains thirteen books. His death in 430 prevented him from reviewing the letters and homilies.

21. Augustine can, nonetheless, be surprisingly frank about things he wrote; for instance, he said that his *De immortalitate animae* "is so obscure that it wearies my mind when it is read and I scarcely understand it myself" (*Retractationes* I, 5, 1: CCL 57, 16: "sic obscurus est, ut fatiget cum legitur etiam intentionem meam uixque intelligatur a me ipso").

22. *Ibid.* II, 6 (32), 1: CCL 59, 94: "A primo usque ad decimum de me scripti sunt, in tribus ceteris de scripturis sanctis, ab eo quod scriptum est: *In principio fecit Deus caelum et terram,* usque ad sabbati requiem."

23. See Pierre Courcelle, *Recherches sur les Confessions de saint Augustin* (Paris: de Boccard, 1950; 2nd ed. 1968), pp. 23-25. In *Augustine: Confessions.* vol. III. *Commentary Books 8-13,* p. 261, James J. O'Donnell points out that Augustine fulfills his promise in his allegorical interpretation of the six days of creation.

24. *Confessiones* XI, 2, 3: CCL 27, 195: "Confitear tibi quidquid inuenero in libris tuis…et considerem mirabilia de lege tua ab usque principio, in quo fecisti caelum et terram, usque ad regnum tecum perpetuum sanctae ciuitatis tuae."

25. Shortly after his baptism and return to Africa, Augustine wrote *De Genesi contra Manichaeos,* to refute the Manichaean objections to the Genesis account of creation. In 393 he began a literal commentary of Genesis which he never completed, *De Genesi ad litteram liber imperfectus.* Between 401 and 415 he wrote his large commentary on Genesis in twelve books, *De Genesi ad litteram,* and in Book Eleven of *De ciuitate Dei* he again commented on the opening chapters of Genesis. In the beginning of the first book of *Contra aduersarium legis et prophetarum,* written in 419 or 420, there is, I have argued, a sixth commentary on Genesis; see "Problems with 'The Beginning' in Augustine's Sixth Commentary on Genesis," *The University of Dayton Review* 22 (1994), 55-67.

26. Since Genesis 1:1 tells of the creation of a heaven before all mention of days, Augustine distinguishes that heaven from the heaven created on the second day. He identifies the first heaven with "the heaven of heaven" mentioned in Psalm 113:16 and takes the heaven made on the second day as the heaven of this earth. Augustine, then, interprets "the heaven of heaven" made before all time as the spiritual creation which, it seems, included the angels and human souls before the fall. On this difficult but fascinating topic, see Jean Pépin, "Recherches sur le sens et l'orgines de l'expression 'coelum coeli' dans les Confessions de saint Augustin," *Archivum Latinitatis Medii Aevi* (*Bulletin du Cange*) 23 (1953), 185-274; A. Hilary Armstrong, "Spiritual or Intelligible Matter in Plotinus and St. Augustine," *Augustinus Magister* I, pp. 276-83; and Robert J. O'Connell's chapter, "The Soul's Eternal Home," in *St. Augustine's Confessions*, pp. 145-57.

27. See *Confessiones* XI, 5, 7-6, 8: CCL 27, 197-98.

28. *Ibid.* XI, 10, 12: CCL 27, 200: "Quid faciebat deus, antequam faceret caelum et terram?"

29. *Ibid.* XI, 30, 40: CCL 27, 215: "Quid ei uenit in mentem, ut aliquid faceret, cum antea numquam aliquid fecerit?"

30. *Ibid.* VII, 1, 1: CCL 27, 92: "et te incorruptibilem et inuiolabilem et incommutabilem totis medullis credebam, quia nesciens, unde et quomodo, plane tamen uidebam et certus eram id, quod corrumpi potest, deterius esse quam id quod non potest, et quod

uiolari non potest, incunctanter praeponebam uiolabili, et quod nullam patitur mutationem, melius esse quam id quod mutari potest."

31. *Epistula* 18 2: CSEL 34/1, 45: "Est natura per locos et tempora mutabilis, ut corpus, et est natura per locos nullo modo, sed tantum per tempora etiam ipsa mutabilis, ut anima, et est natura, quae nec per locos nec per tempora mutari potest, hoc deus est."

32. *Ibid.*: "Quod hic insinuaui quoquo modo mutabile, creatura dicitur; quod inmutabile, creator."

33. *Confessiones* XI, 12, 14: CCL 27, 201: "Respondeo non illud, quod quidam respondisse perhibetur ioculariter eludens quaestionis uiolentiam: 'Alta,' inquit, 'scrutantibus gehennas parabat.'"

34. The African clergy were not merely philosophically uneducated, but seem to have needed quite basic instruction in the Creed, at least if we can judge by those of a few decades later. Shortly after his ordination to the priesthood, Augustine's bishop, Valerius, arranged for him to preach to a synod of African bishops gathered in 393 in Hippo, though at that period priests did not ordinarily preach at all, much less to bishops. Augustine's talk to the synod, his *De fide et symbolo*, indicates by its simple and clear presentation of the articles of the Creed that he thought that the bishops of Africa needed rather rudimentary instruction in the faith.

35. The African church was still very much under the influence of the third-century African theologian

Tertullian. Though he did not quite say, "Credo, quia absurdum," as is often supposed, he did say, "Et mortuus est dei filius; credible est, quia ineptum est. Et sepultus resurrexit; certum est, quia impossibile (The Son of God died; it is entirely credible, because it is absurd; and after his burial he rose again; it is certain, because it is impossible)" (*De carne Christi* V, 4: CCL 2, 881). Christopher Stead argues that Tertullian himself did not intend his paradoxical statements in a literal sense and that they represent "a version of the argument that 'no one would dare to invent so improbable a story'…" (*Philosophy in Christian Antiquity* [Cambridge: Cambridge Univ. Press, 1994], p. 111). Whatever Tertullian's intentions may have been, he was understood — and understood, I think, quite correctly — to have had little use for philosophy.

36. See *De utilitate credendi* I, 2: CSEL 25, 4: "Nosti enim, Honorate, non aliam ob causam nos in tales homines incidisse, nisi quod se dicebant terribili auctoritate separata mera et simplici ratione eos, qui se audire uellent, introducturos ad Deum et errore omni liberaturos."

37. *Ibid.*: "Quid enim me aliud cogebat annos fere nouem spreta religione, quae mihi puerulo a parentibus insita erat, homines illos sequi ac diligenter audire, nisi quod nos superstitione terreri et fidem nobis ante rationem imperari dicerent, se autem nullum premere ad fidem nisi prius discussa et enodata ueritate? Quis non his pollicitationibus inliceretur, praesertim adulescentis animus cupidus ueri, etiam nonnullorum in schola doctorum hominum disputationibus superbus et

garrulus, qualem me tunc illi inuenerunt, spernentem scilicet quasi aniles fabulas et ab eis promissum apertum et sincerum uerum tenere atque haurire cupientem?"

38. See also *ibid.* IX, 21: CSEL 25, 26: "Profitentur hoc omnes haeretici, negare non possum, sed ita, ut eis, quos inlectant, rationem se de obscurissimis rebus polliceantur reddituros, eoque catholicam maxime criminantur, quod illis, qui ad eam ueniunt, praecipitur, ut credant, se autem non iugum credendi inponere, sed docendi fontem aperire gloriantur."

39. The fact that Augustine left the Catholic Church for the Manichees, precisely because he could not find answers to his questions from the Church need not be taken as indicative of an excessive rationalism of Augustine's part. There are some questions which, once posed, must be answered, or one is left with the alternative of "believing" a contradiction. Despite the example supposedly set by the White Queen, practice at believing impossible things is of no avail.

40. For a good introduction to the Manichees, see Peter Brown's chapter on "Manichaeism" in *Augustine of Hippo*, pp. 46-60, or Gerald Bonner's chapters on "The Manichaean Religion" and "Augustine's Polemic against the Manichees" in *St. Augustine of Hippo: Life and Controversies* (London: SCM Press, 1963), pp. 157-236.

41. See Robert J. O'Connell, "On Augustine's 'First Conversion' *Factus Erectior* (*De Beata Vita* 4)," *Augustinian Studies* 17 (1986), 15-29, for a persuasive

argument that, even after his conversion in 386, Augustine looked back upon his joining the Manichees as an improvement over his condition prior to joining them.

42. For the history of the concept of "spirit," see Gerard Verbeke, *L'évolution de la doctrine du pneuma du stoïcisme à s. Augustin* (Louvain: Desclée de Brouwer, 1945), as well as François Masai, "Les conversions de S. Augustin et les débuts du spiritualisme en Occident," *Le Moyen Age* 67 (1961), 1-40. Also see my "Saint Augustine as Philosopher: The Birth of Christian Metaphysics," *Augustinian Studies* 23 (1992), 7-32.

43. See, for example, S. T. Georgiou, *The Last Transfiguration: The Quest for Spiritual Illumination in the Life and Times of Saint Augustine* (Grand Rapids, MI: Phanes Press, 1994), pp. 99-100, where the author claims that Augustine's concept of a bodiless deity was found in the Johannine statement that God is spirit (Jn 4:24). Similarly, in *Saint Augustin et Cicéron* (Paris: Études augustiniennes, 1958) I, p. 110, Maurice Testard, while noting some Christian beliefs that Augustine always held, says, "Or, d'autres croyances, aussi fondamentales dans la foi chrétienne, semblent faire totalement défaut à Augustin; nul doute cependant qu'il les reçut: je pense à la question de la nature spirituelle de Dieu et de l'âme."

44. The need first to discover what evil is before asking from where it comes is reflected in Augustine's admission that he was asking in the wrong way: *Confessiones* VII, 5, 7: CCL 27, 96: "Et quaerebam, unde malum, et male quaerebam...." See Plotinus, *Ennead* I, 8, 1,

ll. 1-5; Armstrong, I, p. 278, where he makes the same point: Οἱ ζητοῦντες, πόθεν τὰ κακά, εἴτ᾽ οὖν εἰς τὰ ὄντα εἴτε περὶ γένος τῶν ὄντων παρελήλυθεν, ἀρχὴν ἂν προσήκουσαν τῆς ζητήσεως ποιοῖντο, εἰ τί ποτ᾽ ἐστὶ τὸ κακὸν καὶ ἡ κακοῦ φύσις πρότερον ὑποθεῖντο.

45. See *Confessiones* V, 10, 19-20: CCL 27, 68: "Et quoniam cum de deo meo cogitare uellem, cogitare nisi moles corporum non noueram — neque enim uidebatur mihi esse quidquam, quod tale non esset — ea maxima et prope sola causa erat ineuitabilis erroris mei. Hinc enim et mali substantiam quandam credebam esse talem...."

46. For this argument see my "The Aim of Augustine's Proof That God Truly Is," *International Philosophical Quarterly* 26 (1986), 253-68, especially p. 259, n. 18. Augustine's Manichaean opponent Fortunatus, asks in *Contra Fortunatum* 5: CSEL 25, 86, whether there is something outside of God or everything is in God: "utrum aliquid sit praeter Deum, an omnia in Deo sunt" — a question which, when applied to evil, entails either that the evil is external to God and limits him or is in God and renders him evil, at least to some extent.

47. *De Genesi contra Manichaeos* I, ii, 3: PL 34, 174: "Quaerunt, in quo principio; et dicunt: Si in principio aliquo temporis fecit Deus coelum et terram, quid agebat antequam faceret coelum et terram?"

48. *Ibid.*: "Et quid ei subito placuit facere, quod nunquam antea fecerat per tempora aeterna?"

49. For the background of this question, see E. Peters, "What Was God Doing Before He Created the Heavens and the Earth?" *Augustinia* 34 (1984), 53-74.

50. *Ibid.*, p. 72.

51. See *Confessiones* XI, 10, 12: CCL 27, 200.

52. *Ibid.* XI, 13, 15: CCL 27, 202: "Id ipsum enim tempus tu feceras, nec praeterire potuerunt tempora, antequam faceres tempora. Si autem ante caelum et terram nullum erat tempus, cur quaeritur, quid tunc faciebas? Non enim erat tunc, ubi non erat tempus."

53. Augustine's problem, it should be noted, is not the problem of the eternity of the world as it was posed for scholastics of the thirteenth century. In confronting the Platonic claim that the soul cannot last forever if it has a temporal beginning, Augustine touches only tangentially upon that question in *De ciuitate dei* X, 31, where he reports that the Platonists distinguished between a beginning in time and a relation of dependence.

54. *Confessiones* XI, 7, 9: CCL 27, 198: "sempiterne dicitur et eo sempiterne dicuntur omnia. Neque enim finitur, quod dicebatur, et dicitur aliud, ut possint dici omnia, sed simul ac sempiterne omnia: alioquin iam tempus et mutatio et non uera aeternitas nec uera immortalitas."

55. *Ibid.* XI, 7, 9: CCL 27, 199: "in quantum quidque non est quod erat et est quod non erat, in tantum moritur

et oritur. Non ergo quidquam uerbi tui cedit atque succedit, quoniam uere immortale atque aeternum...."

56. *Ibid.* XI, 11, 13: CCL 27, 201: "non autem praeterire quidquam in aeterno, sed totum esse praesens; nullum uero tempus totum esse praesens...."

57. *Ibid.* XI, 13, 16: CCL 27, 202: "Nec tu tempore tempora praecedis: alioquin non omnia tempora praecederes. Sed praecedis omnia praeterita celsitudine semper praesentis aeternitatis et superas omnia futura, quia illa futura sunt, et cum uenerint, praeterita erunt; tu autem idem ipse es, et anni tui non deficient. Anni tui nec eunt nec ueniunt: isti enim nostri eunt et ueniunt, ut omnes ueniant. Anni tui omnes simul stant, quoniam stant, nec euntes a uenientibus excluduntur, quia non transeunt: isti autem nostri omnes erunt, cum omnes non erunt. Anni tui dies unus, et dies tuus non cotidie, sed hodie, quia hodiernus tuus non cedit crastino; neque enim succedit hesterno. Hodiernus tuus aeternitas...."

58. The expression "the Selfsame" (*idipsum*) is found in the Psalms, e.g., Psalm 4:9, where the psalmist says, "in pace in idipsum dormiam et requiescam" and Psalm 121:3, where he speaks of "Ierusalem...cujus participatio eius in idipsum." See James Swetnam, "A Note on *In Idipsum* in St. Augustine," *The Modern Schoolman* 30 (1953), 328-33. But the term is virtually a translation of the Plotinian τὸ ταὐτόν, and Augustine clearly interprets it in that sense.

59. *Confessiones* XII, 7, 7: CCL 27, 219: "non es alias aliud et alias aliter, sed id ipsum et id ipsum et id ipsum, sanctus, sanctus, sanctus, dominus deus omnipotens...."

60. *Enarratio in Psalmum* 101, s. 2, 10: CCL 40, 1445: "Non enim aliud anni Dei, et aliud ipse; sed anni Dei, aeternitas Dei est; aeternitas, ipsa Dei substantia est; quae nihil habet mutabile; ibi nihil est praeteritum, quasi iam non sit; nihil est futurum, quasi nondum sit. Non est ibi nisi: Est; non est ibi: Fuit et erit, quia et quod fuit, iam non est; et quod erit, nondum est; sed quidquid ibi est, nonnisi est."

61. Boethius, *De consolatione philosophiae* V, 6, 4: CCL 94, 101: "Aeternitas igitur est interminabilis uitae tota simul et perfecta possessio."

62. See David Balás, *METAOUSIA TOU THEOU: Man's Participation in God's Perfections according to Gregory of Nyssa* (Rome: Herder, 1966), who argues for a clear dependence of Gregory upon Plotinus's concepts of time and eternity. In *Time, Creation and the Continuum: Theories in Antiquity and the Early Middle Ages* (Ithaca: Cornell University Press, 1983), Richard Sorabji points out Gregory of Nyssa's denial of duration in God, especially in his *Contra Eunomium* (p. 123).

63. R. Sorabji, *Time, Creation, and the Continuum,* pp. 114 and 123.

64. Origen, *De principiis* I, 4, 11: SC 252, 138: "Sempiternum uel aeternum proprie dicitur quod

neque initium ut esset habuit, neque cessare umquam potest esse quod est." The citations from the *De principiis* are from *Traité des principes*. vols. I-II., ed. Henri Crouzel and Manlio Simonetti. Sources chrétiennes 252-53 (Paris: Editions du Cerf, 1978).

65. My translation; see *ibid.* II (SC 253, 52, n. 71): "Mais il ne semble pas être parvenu à une notion de l'éternité supprimant clairement la successivité."

66. *Ibid.* I, 4, 3: SC 252, 168-70: "Hic est bonus deus et benignus omnium pater, simul et εὐεργετικὴ δύναμις et δημιουργική, id est bene faciendi uirtus et creandi ac prouidendi. Quas uirtutes dei absurdum simul et impium est putare uel ad momentum aliquod aliquando fuisse otiosas…. Et ideo nullum prorsus momentum sentiri potest, quo non uirtus illa benefica bene fecerit…. Et per hoc consequens uidetur quod neque conditor neque beneficus neque prouidens deus aliquando non fuerit." The translation is mine, though I have consulted the French translation in SC 252.

67. In their notes Crouzel and Simonetti comment, "Supposer que Dieu n'est pas actif de toute éternité, c'est prétendre qu'il a été empêché par des forces extérieures ou qu'il n'a pas voulu agir: cela est incompatible avec sa toute-puissance et son immutabilité. Mais admettre que Dieu est actif de toute éternité, c'est accepter que la création lui soit coéternelle, affirmation contraire à la regle de foi" (*ibid.* II: SC 253, 80).

68. *Ibid.* I, 4, 4: SC 252, 170: "Sed rursum in hoc humana intelligentia hebetatur atque constringitur, quomodo

possit intellegi semper ex quo deus est fuisse etiam
creaturas et sine initio, ut ita dixerim, substitisse eas,
quae utique sine dubio creatae esse atque a deo factae
credendae sunt."

69. *Ibid.*: "In hac igitur sapientia, quae semper erat cum
patre, descripta semper inerat ac formata conditio, et
numquam erat quando eorum, quae futura erant,
praefiguratio apud sapientiam non erat."

70. *Ibid.* SC 253, 80: "La création coéternelle à Dieu c'est
le Monde Intelligible, contentant les plans de la création
et les germes des êtres à venir, et s'identifiant avec le
Fils en tant qu'il est Sagesse."

71. Sorabji cites a passage from Origen's *Commentary on
John* in which he applies temporal extendedness to
God, "For there is no evening of God, I think, since
there is no morning either, but the time (*chronos*)
stretching out along with (*sumparekteinōn*) his
uncreated and everlasting life, if I may so put it, is for
him the today in which the Son has been begotten"
(1.29 [31], 204; cited from Sorabji, p. 123).

72. *Ibid.* p. 123.

73. D. O'Brien, "Temps et éternité dans la philosophie
grecque," in *Mythes et représentations du temps,* ed.
Dorian Tiffeneau (Paris: Éditions du centre national
de la recherche scientifique, 1985), pp. 59-85.

74. *Ennead* III, 7, 5, ll. 25-28; Armstrong, III, pp. 312-
13: Καὶ εἴ τις οὕτω τὸν αἰῶνα λέγοι ζωὴν ἄπειρον

ἤδη τῷ πᾶσαν εἶναι καὶ μηδὲν ἀναλίσκειν αὐτῆς
τῷ μὴ παρεληλυθέναι μηδ᾽ αὖ μέλλειν — ἤδη γὰρ
οὐκ ἂν εἴη πᾶσα — ἐγγὺς ἂν εἴη τοῦ ὁρίζεσθαι.

75. *Ibid.* III, 7, 6, ll. 7-22; Armstrong, III, pp. 312-15:
ἀλλ᾽ ἡ περὶ τὸ ἕν τοῦ ὄντος ζωὴ ὡσαύτως, τοῦτο
ὃ ζητοῦμεν· καὶ τὸ οὕτω μένειν αἰὼν εἶναι.... Τὸ
γὰρ ἀληθῶς εἶναί ἐστι τὸ οὐδέποτε μὴ εἶναι οὐδ᾽
ἄλλως εἶναι· τοῦτο δὲ ὡσαύτως εἶναι· τοῦτο δὲ
ἀδιαφόρως εἶναι. Οὐκ ἔχει οὖν ὁτιοῦν [τὸ] ἄλλο
καὶ ἄλλο, οὐδ᾽ ἄρα διαστήσεις, οὐδ᾽ ἐξελίξεις,
οὐδὲ προάξεις, οὐδὲ παρατενεῖς, οὐδ᾽ ἄρα οὐδὲ
πρότερον αὐτοῦ οὐδέ τι ὕστερον λαβεῖν ἔχεις. Εἰ
οὖν μήτε πρότερον μήτε ὕστερον περὶ αὐτό, τὸ δ᾽
«ἔστι» ἀληθέστατον τῶν περὶ αὐτὸ καὶ αὐτό, καὶ
οὕτω δέ, ὅτι ἐστὶν ὡς οὐσίᾳ ἢ τῷ ζῆν, πάλιν αὖ
ἥκει ἡμῖν τοῦτο, ὃ δὴ λέγομεν, ὁ αἰών.

76. In my "St. Augustine's Use of 'Manens in Se,'" pp.
304-306, I pointed to possible Plotinian sources for
the phrase, "*manens in se*," which phrase Augustine
clearly found in Wisdom 7:27b.

77. *Ennead* III, 7, 3, ll. 13-23; Armstrong, III, pp. 302-
05: καὶ οὐδέποτε ἄλλο καὶ οὐκ ἐξ ἄλλου εἰς ἄλλο
νόησιν ἢ ζωήν, ἀλλὰ τὸ ὡσαύτως καὶ ἀεὶ
ἀδιαστάτως, ταῦτα πάντα ἰδὼν αἰῶνα εἶδεν ἰδὼν
ζωὴν μένουσαν ἐν τῷ αὐτῷ ἀεὶ παρὸν τὸ πᾶν
ἔχουσαν, ἀλλ᾽ οὐ νῦν μὲν τόδε, αὖθις δ᾽ ἕτερον,
ἀλλ᾽ ἅμα τὰ πάντα, καὶ οὐ νῦν μὲν ἕτερα, αὖθις
δ᾽ ἕτερα, ἀλλὰ τέλος ἀμερές, οἷον ἐν σημείῳ ὁμοῦ
πάντων ὄντων καὶ οὔποτε εἰς ῥύσιν προϊόντων,

ἀλλὰ μένοντος ἐν τῷ αὐτῷ ἐν αὐτῷ οὐ μὴ
μεταβάλλοντος, ὄντος δ᾽ ἐν τῷ παρόντι ἀεί, ὅτι
οὐδὲν αὐτοῦ παρῆλθεν οὐδ᾽ αὖ γενήσεται, ἀλλὰ
τοῦτο ὅπερ ἔστι, τοῦτο καὶ ὄντος.

78. Augustine's words in *Confessiones* XI, 14, 17: CCL
27, 202: "Quid est ergo tempus? Si nemo ex me
quaerat, scio; si quaerenti explicare uelim, nescio," call
to mind Plotinus's more prosaic words about eternity
and time in *Ennead* III, 7, 1, ll. 5-9; Armstrong III,
pp. 296-97: ...ἐναργές τι παρ᾽ αὐτοῖς περὶ αὐτῶν
ἐν ταῖς ψυχαῖς ἔχειν πάθος νομίζομεν λέγοντές
τε ἀεὶ παρ᾽ ἅπαντα ὀνομάζοντες. Πειρώμενοι
μὴν εἰς ἐπίστασιν αὐτῶν ἰέναι καὶ οἷον ἐγγὺς
προσελθεῖν πάλιν αὖ ταῖς γνώμαις ἀπορούντες:
"...we think that we have a clear and distinct experience of them in our own souls, as we are always
speaking of them and using their names on every
occasion. Of course, when we try to concentrate on
them and, so to speak, get close to them, we find again
that our thought runs into difficulties...."

79. *Confessiones* XI, 14, 17: CCL 27, 203: "Duo ergo illa
tempora, praeteritum et futurum, quomodo sunt,
quando et praeteritum iam non est et futurum nondum
est? Praesens autem si semper esset praesens nec in
praeteritum transiret, non iam esset tempus, sed
aeternitas. Si ergo praesens, ut tempus sit, ideo fit, quia
in praeteritum transit, quomodo et hoc esse dicimus,
cui causa, ut sit, illa est, quia non erit, ut scilicet non
uere dicamus tempus esse, nisi quia tendit non esse?"
In *Was Ist Zeit?*, Flasch points out that Aristotle
mentioned this problem in *Physics* IV, 217b31-33,

which was further developed by the Skeptics and Stoics. See John F. Callahan, *Augustine and the Greek Philosophers*, The St. Augustine Lecture 1964 (Villanova: Villanova Univ. Press, 1967), p. 87.

80. "En somme, sauf peut être *tempus*, Augustin n'a pas eu de nom pour le monde de la γένεσις" ("Notes sur l'être et le temps chez saint Augustin," *Recherches augustiniennes* 2 [1962], 205-23, here 212).

81. See, for example, *In Iohannis euangelium tractatus* 38, 10: CCL 36, 343, where he comments on Christ's words, "Nisi credideritis quia ego sum," and asks, "Quid enim non est eorum quae fecisti? numquid caelum non est? numquid terra non est? numquid non sunt ea quae in terra et in caelo sunt? numquid homo ipse cui loqueris non est? numquid angelus quem mittis non est? Si omnia sunt haec quae per te facta sunt, quid est quod tibi proprium quiddam tenuisti ipsum esse, quod aliis non dedisti, ut tu solus esses?" And he answers his own question, "Quid sit ipsum esse, dicat cordi, intus dicat, intus loquatur; homo interior audiat, mens capiat uere esse; est enim semper eodem modo esse. Res enim aliqua, quaelibet omnino,…prorsus qualicumque excellentia, si mutabilis est, non uere est; non enim est ibi uerum esse, ubi est et non esse."

82. Some see the whole point of Book Eleven as underscoring the contingency of our existence and dependence upon God. "Das elfte Buch der Bekenntnisse ist nicht in erster Linie eine systematische Abhandlung zum viel verhandelten Thema: 'Schöpfung, Ewigkeit

und Zeit' (das ist es erst in zweiter Linie). Es ist primär der Versuch, sich persönlich über die Art der menschlichen und der göttlichen Seinsweise einige Klarheit zu verschaffen." E. P. Meijering, *Augustin über Schöpfung, Ewigkeit und Zeit: Das elfte Buch der Bekenntnisse* (Leiden: E. J. Brill, 1979), p. 115.

83. *Confessiones* XI, 15, 20: CCL 27, 204: "Si quid intellegitur temporis, quod in nullas iam uel minutissimas momentorum partes diuidi possit, id solum est, quod praesens dicatur; quod tamen ita raptim a futuro in praeteritum transuolat, ut nulla morula extendatur."

84. *Ibid.* XI, 15, 20: CCL 27, 204: "praesens autem nullum habet spatium."

85. *Ibid.*: "...clamat praesens tempus longum se esse non posse."

86. *Ibid.* XI, 28, 37: CCL 27, 214: "Et quis negat praesens tempus carere spatio, quia in puncto praeterit?"

87. *Ibid.* XI, 16, 21: CCL 27, 205: "Sed praetereuntia metimur tempora, cum sentiendo metimur; praeterita uero, quae iam non sunt, aut futura, quae nondum sunt, quis metiri potest, nisi forte audebit quis dicere metiri posse quod non est?"

88. *Ibid.* XI, 17, 22: CCL 27, 205: "Qui narrant praeterita, non utique uera narrarent, si animo illa non cernerent: quae si nulla essent, cerni omnino non possent. Sunt ergo et futura et praeterita."

89. *Ibid.* XI, 18, 23: CCL 27, 205: "Quamquam praeterita cum uera narrantur, ex memoria proferuntur non res ipsae, quae praeterierunt, sed uerba concepta ex imaginibus earum, quae in animo uelut uestigia per sensus praetereundo fixerunt."

90. *Ibid.* XI, 18, 24: CCL 206: "Cum ergo uideri dicuntur futura, non ipsa, quae nondum sunt, id est quae futura sunt, sed eorum causae uel signa forsitan uidentur; quae iam sunt...."

91. *Ibid.* XI, 20, 26: CCL 27, 206-07: "Quod autem nunc liquet et claret, nec futura sunt nec praeterita, nec proprie dicitur: tempora sunt tria, praeteritum, praesens et futurum, sed fortasse proprie diceretur: tempora sunt tria, praesens de praeteritis, praesens de praesentibus, praesens de futuris. Sunt enim haec in anima tria quaedam et alibi ea non uideo, praesens de praeteritis memoria, praesens de praesentibus con-tuitus, praesens de futuris expectatio."

92. *Ibid.* 207: "Ecce non curo nec resisto nec reprehendo, dum tamen intellegatur quod dicitur, neque id, quod futurum est, esse iam, neque id, quod praeteritum est."

93. *Ibid.* XI, 21, 27: CCL 27, 207: "Respondeam: 'scio, quia metimur, nec metiri quae non sunt possumus, et non sunt praeterita uel futura.'"

94. *Ibid.*: "Praesens uero tempus quomodo metimur, quando non habet spatium?"

95. *Ibid.*: "Vtrum in futuro, unde praeterit? Sed quod nondum est, non metimur. An in praesenti, qua praeterit? Sed nullum spatium non metimur. An in praeterito, quo praeterit? Sed quod iam non est, non metimur."

96. *Ibid.* XI, 22, 28: CCL 27, 208: "Da quod amo: amo enim, et hoc tu dedisti."

97. The identity of this person is not clear, though Augustine may have had in mind Plato who expressed such a view in *Timaeus* 39cd, which Augustine could have known in Latin translation. See Flasch, *Was ist Zeit?*, pp. 370-72 for a discussion of possible sources of this idea. Flasch regards the view as a commonplace among ancient authors and sees no need to appeal to the Greek Fathers as Callahan does; see John F. Callahan, "Basil of Caesarea, a New Source for St. Augustine's Theory of Time," *Harvard Studies in Classical Philology* 63 (1958), 437-54.

98. See Joshua 10:12-14 for the battle of Gibeon. Though Augustine undoubtedly accepted the biblical account as fact, his point about time is not dependent on the occurrence of that marvelous event. John Rist (*Augustine: Ancient Thought Baptized*, p. 7) speaks of Augustine taking from the scriptures the equivalent of the thought experiments of contemporary philosophers. That is, it is sufficient for Augustine's point, I believe, that one be able to think of the sun standing still while time continues in order to realize that the movement of the sun does not constitute time. *Confessiones* XI, 23, 30: CCL 27, 209: "Nemo ergo mihi dicat caelestium

corporum motus esse tempora, quia et cuiusdam uoto
cum sol stetisset, ut uictoriosum proelium perageret,
sol stabat, sed tempus ibat. Per suum quippe spatium
temporis, quod ei sufficeret, illa pugna gesta atque
finita est."

99. *Confessiones* XI, 23, 30: CCL 27, 209: "Video igitur
tempus quandam esse distentionem. Sed uideo? An
uidere mihi uideor? Tu demonstrabis, lux, ueritas."

100. *Ibid.* XI, 24, 31: CCL 27, 210: "Iubes ut approbem,
si quis dicat tempus esse motum corporis? Non iubes.
Nam corpus nullum nisi in tempore moueri audio: tu
dicis. Ipsum autem corporis motum tempus esse non
audio: non tu dicis.... Cum itaque aliud sit motus
corporis, aliud, quo metimur quandiu sit, quis non
sentiat, quid horum potius tempus dicendum sit?"

101. *Ibid.*: "Nam si et uarie corpus aliquando mouetur,
aliquando stat, non solum motum eius, sed etiam
statum tempore metimur.... Non est ergo tempus
corporis motus."

102. *Ibid.* XI, 26, 33: CCL 27, 211: "Nonne tibi confitetur
anima mea confessione ueridica metiri me tempora?
Itane, deus meus, metior et quid metiar nescio. Metior
motum corporis tempore. Item ipsum tempus nonne
metior?"

103. *Ibid.*: "Inde mihi uisum est nihil esse aliud tempus
quam distentionem: sed cuius rei, nescio, et mirum, si
non ipsius animi."

104. *Ibid.* VIII, 10, 24: CCL 27, 128: "Si ergo pariter delectent omnia simulque uno tempore, nonne diuersae uoluntates distendunt cor hominis, dum deliberatur, quod potissimum arripiamus?" See *St. Augustine's Confessions*, 2 vols., tr. William Watts (Cambridge, MA: Harvard Univ. Press, 1961), I, p. 455, and *Saint Augustine: Confessions*, tr. Henry Chadwick (Oxford: Oxford Univ. Press, 1991), p. 150.

105. See *De uera religione* 30, 56: CCL 32, 223, where Augustine contrasts things which are beautiful in places and times with the equality and unity known only to the mind which "nec loco tumida est nec instabilis tempore."

106. See *De Genesi contra Manichaeos* II, 5, 6: PL 32, 199, where Augustine describes the soul's fall through pride in terms of a swelling into external things: "in exteriora per superbiam tumescens...."

107. *De quantitate animae* 14, 24: CSEL 89, 160: "Tumor enim non absurde appellatur corporis magnitudo."

108. *Ibid.* 19, 33: CSEL 89, 172: "Nam ut in corpore tria sunt genera incrementorum, unum necessarium,... alterum superfluum,...tertium noxium, quod cum accidit, tumor vocatur...."

109. Though I suspect διάστασις in Plotinus's discussion of time has the neutral meaning of "extension," Liddell and Scott give under its first meaning various medical terms, such as the separation of bones (with ὀστέων), the swelling of veins (with φλεβῶν), a splitting headache (with κεφαλῆς), or a retching (with κενεή).

110. *Confessiones* XI, 29, 39: CCL 27, 214: "ecce distentio est uita mea, et me suscepit dextera tua in domino meo, mediatore filio hominis inter te unum et nos multos, in multis per multa...."

111. *Ibid.*: "et a ueteribus diebus conligar sequens unum, praeterita oblitus, non in ea quae futura et transitura sunt, sed in ea quae ante sunt non distentus, sed extentus...." Here and in the following quotation Augustine paraphrases Philippians 3:12-14.

112. *Ibid.* 214-15: "...non secundum distentionem, sed secundum intentionem sequor ad palmam supernae uocationis, ubi audiam uocem laudis et contempler delectationem tuam nec uenientem nec praetereuntem."

113. *Ibid.* 215: "Nunc uero anni mei in gemitibus, et tu solacium meum, domine, pater meus aeternus es; at ego in tempora dissilui, quorum ordinem nescio, et tumultuosis uarietatibus dilaniantur cogitationes meae, intima uiscera animae meae, donec in te confluam purgatus et liquidus igne amoris tui." Robert J. O'Connell argues that the verb "*dissilui*" should be translated so as to convey that the soul has leapt apart into times. See *St. Augustine's Confessions*, p. 143.

114. Henri-Irénée Marrou, *L'ambivalence du temps de l'histoire chez saint Augustin* (Montréal-Paris: Institut d'études médiévales, 1950).

115. *De uera religione* 24, 45: CCL 32, 215: "In temporalia deuenimus et eorum amore ab aeternis impedimur."

116. *Ibid.* 22, 43: CCL 32, 214: "Huc accedit, quod carminis non sumus partes, saeculorum uero partes damnatione facti sumus."

117. *Ibid.* 35, 65: CCL 32, 230: "Loca offerunt quod amemus, tempora surripiunt quod amamus."

118. *Sermo* 124, 20: PL 38, 688: "A prima infantia usque ad decrepitam senectutem, breve spatium est.... Hesternum diem nemo revocat: hodiernus crastino urgetur, ut transeat.... Et modo cum loquimur, utique transimus. Verba currunt, et horae volant: sic aetas nostra, sic actus nostri, sic honores nostri, sic miseria nostra, sic ista felicitas nostra. Totum transit."

119. *Confessiones* II, 10, 18: CCL 27, 26: "Defluxi abs te ego et erraui, deus meus, nimis deuius ab stabilitate tua in adulescentia et factus sum mihi regio egestatis."

120. *Epistula* 7, 1: CSEL 34/1, 14: "Qui non adtendunt illam uisionem esse praeteritam, quia haec aliquando mente uidimus; a quibus quia defluximus et aliter alia uidere coepimus, ea nos reminiscendo reuisere, id est per memoriam."

121. *Confessiones* X, 29, 40: CCL 27, 176: "Per continentiam quippe colligimur et redigimur in unum, a quo in multa defluximus."

122. *Ibid.* XIII, 8, 9: CCL 27, 245: "Defluxit angelus, defluxit anima hominis et indicauerunt abyssum uniuersae spiritalis creaturae...."

123. *In Iohannis euangelium tractatus* 31, 5: CCL 36, 296: "Denique ubi uenit plenitudo temporis, uenit et ille qui nos liberaret a tempore." See also *Sermo* 340A, 5: *Miscellanea Agostiniana* (Rome, 1931) I, 567: "Venit humilis creator noster, creatus inter nos: qui fecit nos, qui factus est propter nos: deus ante tempora, homo in tempore, ut hominem liberaret a tempore. Venit sanare tumorem nostrum magnus medicus." See also my "*Vocans temporales*," pp. 29-47.

124. *In Iohannis euangelium tractatus* 31, 5: CCL 36, 296: "Liberati enim a tempore, uenturi sumus ad aeternitatem illam, ubi non est tempus...."

125. *Ennead* III, 7, 11, ll. 42-48; Armstrong, III, pp. 340-41: Διάστασις οὖν ζωῆς χρόνον εἶχε καὶ τὸ πρόσω ἀεὶ τῆς ζωῆς χρόνον ἔχει ἀεὶ καὶ ἡ παρελθοῦσα ζωὴ χρόνον ἔχει παρεληλυθότα. Εἰ οὖν χρόνον τις λέγοι ψυχῆς ἐν κινήσει μεταβατικῇ ἐξ ἄλλου εἰς ἄλλον βίον ζωὴν εἶναι, ἆρ᾽ ἂν δοκοῖ τι λέγειν; Εἰ γὰρ αἰών ἐστι ζωὴ ἐν στάσει καὶ τῷ αὐτῷ καὶ ὡσαύτως καὶ ἄπειρος ἤδη, εἰκόνα δὲ δεῖ τοῦ αἰῶνος τόν χρόνον εἶναι...ἀντὶ μὲν ζωῆς τῆς ἐκεῖ ἄλλην δεῖ ζωὴν...λέγειν εἶναι....

126. *Ibid.*, ll. 51-53; Armstrong, III, pp. 340-43: ἀντὶ δὲ ταὐτότητος καὶ τοῦ ὡσαύτως καὶ μένοντος τὸ μὴ μένον ἐν τῷ αὐτῷ, ἄλλο δὲ καὶ ἄλλο ἐνεργοῦν, ἀντὶ δὲ ἀδιαστάτου καὶ ἑνὸς εἴδωλον τοῦ ἑνὸς τὸ ἐν συνεχείᾳ ἕν....

127. *De Genesi ad litteram liber imperfectus* 13, 38: CSEL 28/1, 487: "Haec enim nunc dicit tempora, quae

interuallorum distinctione aeternitatem incommutabilem supra se manere significant, ut signum, id est quasi uestigium aeternitatis tempus adpareat." See *Ennead* III, 7, 1, ll. 18-20, where Plotinus cites Plato's *Timaeus* 37D. Also see *De musica* VI, 11, 29: PL 32, 1179: "Ubi nullum est tempus, quia nulla mutabilitas est; et unde tempora fabricantur et ordinantur et modificantur aeternitatem imitantia, dum coeli conversio ad idem redit, et coelestia corpora ad idem revocat, diebusque et mensibus et annis et lustris, caeterisque siderum orbibus, legibus aequalitatis et unitatis et ordinationis obtemperat."

128. *Confessiones* XI, 26, 33: CCL 27, 211: "Tempus metior, scio; sed non metior futurum, quia nondum est, non metior praesens, quia nullo spatio tenditur, non metior praeteritum, quia iam non est. Quid ergo metior? An praetereuntia tempora, non praeterita? Sic enim dixeram."

129. O'Daly seems to hold just the opposite view; he says, "The problem therefore is one of how we can *measure* time: how can a time period have length and how do we know its length?" See Gerard O'Daly, "Augustine on the Measurement of Time: Some Comparisons with Aristotelian and Stoic Texts," in *Neoplatonism and Early Christian Thought*, ed. J. J. Blumenthal and R. A. Markus (London: Variorum, 1981), p. 171.

130. *Confessiones* XI, 27, 34: CCL 27, 212: "Praeteriens enim tendebatur in aliquod spatium temporis, quo metiri posset, quoniam praesens nullum habet spatium."

131. *Ibid.* XI, 27, 36: CCL 27, 213: "In te, anime meus, tempora metior. Noli mihi obstrepere, quod est: noli tibi obstrepere turbis affectionum tuarum. In te, inquam, tempora metior. Affectionem, quam res praetereuntes in te faciunt et, cum illae praeterierint, manet, ipsam metior praesentem, non ea quae praeterierunt, ut fieret; ipsam metior, cum tempora metior."

132. *Ibid.* XI, 28, 37: CCL 27, 213-14: "Quis igitur negat futura nondum esse? Sed tamen iam est in animo expectatio futurorum. Et quis negat praeterita iam non esse? sed tamen adhuc est in animo memoria praeteritorum. Et quis negat praesens tempus carere spatio, quia in puncto praeterit? Sed tamen perdurat attentio, per quam pergat abesse quod aderit."

133. John F. Callahan, *Four Views of Time in Ancient Philosophy* (Cambridge, MA: Harvard Univ. Press, 1948), p. 165.

134. *Ibid.*, p. 176.

135. Robert Jordan, "Time and Contingency in St. Augustine," *Review of Metaphysics* 8 (1955), 394-417, here 400.

136. See Pierre Lachièze-Rey, "Saint Augustin précurseur de Kant dans la théorie de la perception," *Augustinus Magister* I (Paris: Études augustiniennes, 1954), pp. 425-28.

137. Flasch, *Was Ist Zeit?*, p. 389: "Die *attentio* dauert an, *perdurat attentio*, n. 37, 9. Sie hält das Bild der vorübergehenden Gegenstände über Zeitspannen hinweg fest; sie bringt das Erinnerte mit dem Erwarteten in der Gegenwart zusammen; sie verknüpft das zuvor gegenwärtig Gewesene mit dem jetzt Gegenwärtigen. Dies macht die Zerdehntheit der zeitgebenden Seele aus, die ihr Leben nicht in einem einheitlichen Zugleich, sondern im Nacheinander lebt, vgl. Plotin, *Enn* III 7,11…."

138. *Confessiones* XI, 28, 38: CCL 27, 214: "atque distenditur uita huius actionis meae in memoriam propter quod dixi et in expectationem propter quod dicturus sum: praesens tamen adest attentio mea, per quam traicitur quod erat futurum, ut fiat praeteritum…. Et quod in toto cantico, hoc in singulis particulis eius fit atque in singulis syllabis eius, … hoc in tota uita hominis, cuius partes sunt omnes actiones hominis, hoc in toto saeculo filiorum hominum, cuius partes sunt omnes uitae hominum."

139. B. Russell, *Human Knowledge: Its Scope and Limits* (New York: Simon and Schuster, 1948), p. 212.

140. From the time of his second commentary of Genesis, Augustine appealed to Sirach 18:1 to argue for the simultaneous creation of all things. See *De Genesi ad litteram liber imperfectus* VII, 28, as well as his later *De Genesi ad litteram* IV, 33, 52; V, 3, 6; and V, 17, 35. Hence, he would not have been particularly bothered by this form of the objection.

141. Russell is not alone in interpreting Augustine's view of time in this sense. In his recent book Christopher Stead sees Augustine as holding "that time can be understood purely in terms of our consciousness." He admits the originality of the theory and adds that "Augustine seem to be thinking largely in terms of his own consciousness" (*Philosophy in Christian Antiquity*, p. 239).

142. *De ciuitate Dei* XII, 16: CCL 47, 371: "Erat tempus, quando non erat homo."

143. John L. Morrison, "Augustine's Two Theories of Time," *The New Scholasticism* 45 (1971), 600-10. Oddly enough, Morrison seems to think that Augustine's view of time in the *Confessions* is at least at first glance more compatible with his view of history in the *City of God* than his account of time in the latter work.

144. See J. Guitton, *Le temps et l'éternité*, chapters 7 and 8. Guitton says, for example, "Le temps du livre XI est le temps où se distribuent les sensations et où s'ordonne la conscience présente" (p. 326).

145. *De Genesi contra Manichaeos* I, 2, 3: PL 34, 175: "Quomodo enim erat tempus quod Deus non fecerat, cum omnium temporum ipse sit fabricator? Et si tempus cum coelo et terra esse coepit, non potest inveniri tempus quo Deus nondum fecerat coelum et terram."

146. *Ibid.* I, 2, 4: PL 34, 175: "Non enim coaevum Deo mundum istum dicimus, quia non eius aeternitatis est hic mundus, cuius aeternitatis est Deus: mundum

quippe fecit Deus, et sic cum ipsa creatura quam Deus
fecit, tempora esse coeperunt; et ideo dicuntur tempora
aeterna."

147. *Confessiones* XI, 13, 15; see above note 52 for the text.

148. *De ciuitate Dei* XII, 16: CCL 47, 372: "Ubi enim
nulla creatura est, cujus mutabilibus motibus tempora
peraguntur, tempora omnino esse non possunt."

149. *De Genesi ad litteram* V, 5, 12: CSEL 28/1, 145:
"Factae itaque creaturae motibus coeperunt currere
tempora: unde ante creaturam frustra tempora
requiruntur, quasi possint inueniri ante tempora
tempora. Motus enim si nullus esset uel spiritalis uel
corporalis creaturae, quo per praesens praeteritis futura
succederent, nullum esset tempus omnino."

150. *Ibid.*: "Nec sic accipiatur quod dictum est: tempus
a creatura coepit, quasi tempus creatura non sit, cum
sit creaturae motus ex alio in aliud consequentibus
rebus secundum ordinationem administrantis Dei
cuncta quae creavit."

151. J. Cavadini, "Time and Ascent in *Confessiones* XI,"
p. 179, n. 8. Cavadini adds that he does not assume
"that Augustine is even interested in speculating de-
finitively about time itself...." He rejects the idea,
which he attributes to me, that "Book XI is a treatise on
time, that it does intend to define time..." (p. 184, n. 52).

152. Gerard O'Daly, "Augustine on the Measurement of
Time," p. 171. For evidence of this view, O'Daly

refers his readers to another article of his, "Time as *Distentio* and St. Augustine's Exegesis of *Philippians* 3, 12-14," *Révue des études augustiniennes* 23 (1977), 265-71.

153. *Saint Augustine: Confessions*, p. 230, n. 19.

154. See K. Flasch, *Was Ist Zeit?*, pp. 338-41, for a survey of scholarly opinion on whether or not Augustine set out to define time in Book Eleven of the *Confessions* and whether or not he did do so. Flasch himself is most emphatic that Augustine "macht bei der Frage, was die Zeit ist, keinerlei Einschränkung bezüglich der zu erforschenden Sache: Er will wissen, was *die* Zeit ist. Er stellt die *Was*-Frage in der Art der philosophischen Tradition seit Sokrates…. Er unterscheidet weder hier noch im fogenden zwischen objektiver und subjectiver Zeit. Er will allgemein und einschrängslos erforschen, was die Zeit ist" (p. 339).

155. *Confessiones* XI, 31, 41: CCL 27, 215: "Sicut ergo nosti in principio caelum et terram sine uarietate notitiae tuae, ita fecisti in principio caelum et terram sine distentione actionis tuae."

156. C. Stead makes much the same point when he says that "Augustine's psychological treatment of time may serve his purpose of suggesting the relative unreality of time as contrasted with eternity…but in other ways it frustrates his real objective, since he set out with the intention of understanding God's act of creation. But he clearly wishes to present this as a real

event in the past, even though no human being remembers it" (*Philosophy in Christian Antiquity*, p. 240).

157. *Ennead* III, 7, 11, ll. 27-33; Armstrong, pp. 338-39:
οὕτω δὴ καὶ αὐτὴ κόσμον ποιοῦσα αἰσθητὸν
μιμήσει ἐκείνου κινούμενον κίνησιν οὐ τὴν ἐκεῖ,
ὁμοίαν δὲ τῇ ἐκεῖ καὶ ἐθέλουσαν εἰκόνα ἐκείνης
εἶναι, πρῶτον μὲν ἑαυτὴν ἐχρόνησεν ἀντὶ τοῦ
αἰῶνος τοῦτον ποιήσασα· ἔπειτα δὲ καὶ τῷ
γενομένῳ ἔδωκε δουλεύειν χρόνῳ, ἐν χρόνῳ αὐτὸν
πάντα ποιήσασα εἶναι, τὰς τούτου διεξόδους
ἁπάσας ἐν αὐτῷ περιλαβοῦσα.

158. *Ibid.*, ll. 34-36; Armstrong, pp. 338-41: ἐν ἐκείνῃ
γὰρ κινούμενος — οὐ γάρ τις αὐτοῦ τοῦδε τοῦ
παντὸς τόπος ἢ ψυχή — καὶ ἐν τῷ ἐκείνης αὖ
ἐκινεῖτο χρόνῳ.

159. *Ibid.* III, 7, 13, ll. 46-48; Armstrong, pp. 352-53:
Πῶς οὖν πανταχοῦ; Ὅτι κἀκείνη οὐδενὸς
ἀφέστηκε τοῦ κόσμου μέρους, ὥσπερ οὐδ᾽ ἡ ἐν
ἡμῖν οὐδενὸς ἡμῶν μέρους.

160. *Ibid.* ll. 66-69; Armstrong, pp. 354-55: Ἆρ᾽ οὖν καὶ
ἐν ἡμῖν χρόνος; Ἢ ἐν ψυχῇ τῇ τοιαύτῃ πάσῃ καὶ
ὁμοειδῶς ἐν πάσῃ καὶ αἱ πᾶσαι μία. Διὸ οὐ
διασπασθήσεται ὁ χρόνος· ἐπεὶ οὐδ᾽ ὁ αἰὼν ὁ κατ᾽
ἄλλο ἐν τοῖς ὁμοειδέσι πᾶσιν.

161. Cf. A. Solignac, "Notes complémentaires," in *Les
Confessions*. Livres VIII-XIII. Bibliothèque augustin-
ienne 14 (Paris: Études augustiniennes, 1962), p. 590.

162. "The World-Soul and Time," pp. 91-92.

163. In *Was Ist Zeit?*, pp. 192-95, K. Flasch summarizes
the views of medieval authors and claims that no
medieval authors found in Augustine a distinction
between a subjective and an objective time and that
many took the soul that produces time to be the world-
soul. For further confirmation of these claims, see U.
Jenk's *Aristoteles contra Augustinum. Zur Frage nach dem
Verhältnis von Zeit und Seele bei den antiken Aristoteles-
kommentatoren, im arabischen Aristotelismus und im 13.
Jarhhundert* (Amsterdam: B. R. Grüner, 1994).

164. *De ordine* II, 11, 30: CCL 29, 124: "Ratio est mentis
motio ea, quae discuntur, distinguendi et conectendi
potens, qua duce uti ad deum intellegendum uel
ipsam quae aut in nobis aut usque quaque est animam
rarissimum omnino genus hominum potest non ob
aliud, nisi quia in istorum sensuum negotia progresso
redire in semet ipsum cuique difficile est." See Vernon
J. Bourke, "The Problem of a World Soul," chapter six
in his *Wisdom from St. Augustine* (Houston: Center
for Thomistic Studies, 1984), pp. 78-90, for a discussion of many of the relevant texts. The chapter is a
revision of his article, "St. Augustine and the Cosmic
Soul," *Giornale de Metafisica* 9 (1954), 431-40.

165. *De immortalitate animae* 15, 24: CSEL 89, 125-26:
"Hoc autem ordine intelligitur a summa essentia
speciem corpori per animam tribui, qua est, in quan-
tumcumque est. Per animam ergo corpus subsistit et
eo ipso est, quo animatur, sive universaliter, ut mundus,
sive particulariter, ut unumquodque animal intra

mundum…. Nec invenitur aliquid quod sit inter summam vitam, quae sapientia et veritas est incommutabilis, et id quod ultimum vivificatur, id est corpus, nisi vivificans anima."

166. *Retractationes* I, 5, 3: CCL 57, 17: "… hoc totum prorsus temere dictum est."

167. *Ibid.* I, 11, 4: CCL 57, 35: "Sed animal esse istum mundum, sicut Plato sensit aliique philosophi plurimi, nec ratione certa indagare potui, nec diuinarum scripturarum auctoritate persuaderi posse cognoui."

168. *Ibid.*: "Unde tale aliquid a me dictum quo id accipi possit, etiam in libro de inmortalitate animae temere dictum notaui, non quia hoc falsum esse confirmo, sed quia nec uerum esse conprehendo, quod sit animal mundus."

169. *Ibid.*: "Esse tamen spiritalem uitalemque uirtutem, etiam si non sit animal mundus, quae uirtus in angelis sanctis ad decorandum atque administrandum mundum deo seruit et a quibus non intellegitur, rectissime creditur."

170. *Ibid.*: "Hoc sane inconcusse retinendum esse non dubito, deum nobis non esse istum mundum, siue anima eius ulla siue nulla sit, quia si ulla est, ille qui eam fecit est deus noster, si autem nulla est, nullorum deus potest esse iste, quanto minus noster."

171. *De Genesi ad litteram liber imperfectus* 4, 17: CSEL 28/1, 469: "Potest autem et aliter intellegi, ut spiritum

dei uitalem creaturam, qua uniuersus iste uisibilis atque omnia corpora continentur et mouentur, intellegamus, cui Deus omnipotens tribuit uim quamdam sibi seruiendi ad operandum in iis, quae gignuntur. Qui spiritus cum sit omni corpore aethereo melior, quia omnem uisibilem creaturam omnis inuisibilis creatura antecedit, non absurde spiritus Dei dicitur."

172. *De consensu euangelistarum* I, 23, 35: CSEL 43, 34: "Utrum autem uniuersa ista corporalis moles, quae mundus appellatur, habeat quandam animam uel quasi animam suam, id est rationalem uitam, qua ita regatur sicut unumquodque animal, magna adque abdita quaestio est, nec adfirmari debet ista opinio nisi conperta, quod uera sit, nec refelli nisi conperta, quod falsa sit."

173. *De quantitate animae* 32, 69: CSEL 89, 217: "Si enim dixero unam esse animam, conturbaberis, quod in altero beata est, in altero misera nec una res simul et beata et misera potest esse. Si unam simul et multas dicam esse, ridebis; nec mihi facile, unde tuum risum comprimam, suppetit. Sin multas tantummodo esse dixero, ipse me ridebo minusque me mihi displicentem quam tibi, perferam."

174. In "The Problem of a World Soul," pp. 78-79, V. Bourke pointed out that a ninth-century controversy over the claim that Augustine held a universal soul for all human beings appealed to this text from *De quantitate animae*. At the insistence of Bishop Odo of Beauvais, Ratramnus of Corbie opposed this interpre-

tation of Augustine in his *De anima*. See Ratramnus
of Corbie, *Liber de anima ad Odonem Bellovacensem*,
ed. D.C. Lambot, O.S.B., *Analecta mediaevalia
namurcensia* 2 (Namur-Lille: Editions Godenne,
1951), p. 159.

175. *De quantitate animae* 32, 68: CSEL 89, 216: "…ani-
mus ad haec intuenda et dispicienda praecolendus est,
ut possis intelligere liquidissime, utrum quod a
quibusdam doctissimis viris dicitur, ita sese habeat,
animam per seipsam nullo modo, sed tamen per
corpus posse partiri." In *Plotin et l'occident* (Louvain:
Spicilegium Sacrum Lovaniense, 1934), pp. 74-75,
Paul Henry claimed that the words, "animam…
partiri," are taken verbatim from Plotinus. See *Ennead*
IV, 2, 1, ll. 73-76: μένει γὰρ μεθ᾽ ἑαυτῆς ὅλη, περὶ
δὲ τὰ σώματα ἐστι μεμερισμένη τῶν σωμάτων
τῷ οἰκείῳ μεριστῷ οὐ δυναμένων αὐτὴν ἀμερίστως
δέξασθαι· ὥστε εἶναι τῶν σωμάτων πάθημα τὸν
μερισμόν, οὔκ αὐτῆς.

176. *De quantitate animae* 30, 61: CSEL 89, 207: "Quid
igitur faciam, quaeso te? Nonne istis rationibus confici
potest, animas nostras non esse in corporibus? Quod
si ita est, nonne ubi sim nescio? Quis enim mihi eripit,
quod ego ipse anima sum?"

177. *De ciuitate Dei* X, 22: CCL 47, 296: "Non enim nisi
peccatis homines separantur a Deo…"; *Confessiones* I,
18, 28: CCL 27, 15-16: "Non enim pedibus aut
spatiis locorum itur abs te aut reditur ad te…." So too,
in *Confessiones* VIII, 8, 19: CCL 27, 125-26: "…non
illuc ibatur nauibus aut quadrigis aut pedibus…. Nam

non solum ire, uerum etiam peruenire illuc nihil erat aliud quam uelle ire, sed uelle fortiter et integre…." In the last two texts Augustine is alluding to *Ennead* I, 6, 8.

178. *Epistula* 9: CSEL 34/1, 20: "Confer te ad animum tuum et illum in deum leua, quantum potes. Ibi enim certius habes et nos non per corporeas imagines, quibus nunc in nostra recordatione uti necesse est, sed per illam cogitationem, qua intellegis non loco esse nos simul."

179. *De uera religione* 47, 91: CCL 32, 247: "Animi autem coniunctio maior est quam locorum aut temporum…."

180. *Confessiones* IV, 6, 11: CCL 27, 45: "Bene quidam dixit de amico suo dimidium animae suae." But in *Retractationes* II, 6 (32), 2: CCL 57, 94, he regrets having said that "anima nostra una quodammodo facta fuerat ex duabus" and that he feared his own death "ne totus ille moreretur, quem multum amaueram."

181. *In Iohannis euangelium tractatus* 18, 4: CCL 36, 181-182: "Si enim caritas quam misit hominibus Deus, de multis hominum cordibus facit cor unum, et multas hominum animas facit animam unam, sicut de credentibus seseque inuicem diligentibus scriptum est in actibus apostolorum: *Erat illis anima una, et cor unum in Deum,* si ergo anima mea et anima tua, cum idem sapimus nosque diligimus, fit anima una, quanto magis Pater Deus et Filius Deus in fonte dilectionis Deus unus est?"

182. *Confessiones* XI, 31, 41: CCL 27, 215: "Certe si est
     tam grandi scientia et praescientia pollens animus, cui
     cuncta praeterita et futura ita nota sint, sicut mihi
     unum canticum notissimum, nimium mirabilis est
     animus iste atque ad horrorem stupendus, quippe
     quem ita non lateat quidquid peractum et quidquid
     reliquum saeculorum est, quemadmodum me non
     latet cantantem illud canticum, quid et quantum eius
     abierit ab exordio, quid et quantum restet ad finem."

183. See K. Flasch, *Was Ist Zeit?*, pp. 407-08.

184. *Confessiones* XI, 31, 41: CCL 27, 215: "Sed absit, ut
     tu, conditor uniuersitatis, conditor animarum et
     corporum, absit, ut ita noueris omnia futura et
     praeterita. Longe tu, longe mirabilius longeque
     secretius."

185. See *Ennead* I, 6, 8, ll. 16-17 and 22-23; Armstrong,
     I, pp. 256-57: Φεύγωμεν δὴ φίλην ἐς πατρίδα....
     Πατρὶς δὴ ἥμιν, ὅθεν παρήθομεν, καὶ πατὴρ ἐκεῖ.

186. "The World-Soul and Time," p. 92.

187. See *Confessiones* XII, 15, 19: CCL 27, 225, where
     Augustine describes the heaven of heaven as: "sublimem
     quandam ... creaturam tam casto amore cohaerentem
     deo uero et uere aeterno, ut, quamuis ei coaeterna non
     sit, in nullam tamen temporum uarietatem et
     uicissitudinem ab illo se resoluat et defluat, sed in eius
     solius ueracissima contemplatione requiescat" and as
     "particeps aeternitatis tuae, quia sine labe in aeternum."
     Though the heaven of heaven has not "flowed down"

into the variations of time, Augustine says of himself, "Defluxi ad ista…" (*ibid.* XII, 10, 10: CCL 27, 221) in contrast with the heaven of heaven which checks its mutability "sine ullo lapsu" and "inhaerendo tibi excedit omnem uolubilem uicissitudinem temporum" (*ibid.* XII, 9, 9: CCL 27, 221). So too, he says, "Defluxit angelus, defluxit anima hominis…" (*ibid.* XIII, 8, 9: CCL 27, 245).

188. *De ciuitate Dei* XIII, 14: CCL 48, 395: "Omnes enim fuimus in illo uno, quando omnes fuimus ille unus, qui per feminam lapsus est in peccatum, quae de illo facta est ante peccatum."

189. Rist, *Augustine: Ancient Thought Baptized*, p. 126.

190. *De gratia Christi et de peccato originali* II, 24, 28: CSEL 42, 187: "In horum ergo duorum hominum causa proprie fides christiana consistit."

About the Aquinas Lecture Series

The Annual St. Thomas Aquinas Lecture Series began at Marquette University in the Spring of 1937. Ideal for classroom use, library additions, or private collections, the Aquinas Lecture Series has received international acceptance by scholars, universities, and libraries. Hardbound in maroon cloth with gold stamped covers. Uniform style and price ($15 each). Some reprints with soft covers. Complete set (60 Titles) (ISBN 0-87462-150-X) receives a 40% discount. New standing orders receive a 30% discount. Regular reprinting keeps all volumes available. Ordering information (purchase orders, checks, and major credit cards accepted):

> Bookmasters Distribution Services
> 1444 U.S. Route 42
> Mansfield OH 44903
> Order Toll-Free (800) 247-6553
> FAX: (419) 281 6883

Editorial Address:
Dr. Andrew Tallon, Director
Marquette University Press
Box 1881
Milwaukee WI 53201-1881
Tel: (414) 288-7298 FAX: (414) 288-3300
Internet: tallona@vms.csd.mu.edu . CompuServe : 73627,1125.

ISBN 0-87462-163-1